# Palgrave Studies in Creativity and Culture

**Series Editors**
Vlad Petre Glăveanu, School of Psychology, Dublin City University, Dublin, Ireland
Brady Wagoner, Communication and Psychology, Aalborg University, Aalborg, Denmark

Both creativity and culture are areas that have experienced a rapid growth in interest in recent years. Moreover, there is a growing interest today in understanding creativity as a socio-cultural phenomenon and culture as a transformative, dynamic process. Creativity has traditionally been considered an exceptional quality that only a few people (truly) possess, a cognitive or personality trait 'residing' inside the mind of the creative individual. Conversely, culture has often been seen as 'outside' the person and described as a set of 'things' such as norms, beliefs, values, objects, and so on. The current literature shows a trend towards a different understanding, which recognises the psycho-socio-cultural nature of creative expression and the creative quality of appropriating and participating in culture. Our new, interdisciplinary series Palgrave Studies in Creativity and Culture intends to advance our knowledge of both creativity and cultural studies from the forefront of theory and research within the emerging cultural psychology of creativity, and the intersection between psychology, anthropology, sociology, education, business, and cultural studies. Palgrave Studies in Creativity and Culture is accepting proposals for monographs, Palgrave Pivots and edited collections that bring together creativity and culture. The series has a broader focus than simply the cultural approach to creativity, and is unified by a basic set of premises about creativity and cultural phenomena.

Alex Urmeneta · Margarida Romero
Editors

# Creative Applications of Artificial Intelligence in Education

*Editors*
Alex Urmeneta
Université Côte D'Azur
Nice, France

Margarida Romero
Université Côte D'Azur
Nice, France

ISSN 2755-4503  ISSN 2755-4511 (electronic)
Palgrave Studies in Creativity and Culture
ISBN 978-3-031-55271-7  ISBN 978-3-031-55272-4 (eBook)
https://doi.org/10.1007/978-3-031-55272-4

© The Editor(s) (if applicable) and The Author(s) 2024. This book is an open access publication.

**Open Access** This book is licensed under the terms of the Creative Commons Attribution 4.0 International License (http://creativecommons.org/licenses/by/4.0/), which permits use, sharing, adaptation, distribution and reproduction in any medium or format, as long as you give appropriate credit to the original author(s) and the source, provide a link to the Creative Commons license and indicate if changes were made.

The images or other third party material in this book are included in the book's Creative Commons license, unless indicated otherwise in a credit line to the material. If material is not included in the book's Creative Commons license and your intended use is not permitted by statutory regulation or exceeds the permitted use, you will need to obtain permission directly from the copyright holder.

The use of general descriptive names, registered names, trademarks, service marks, etc. in this publication does not imply, even in the absence of a specific statement, that such names are exempt from the relevant protective laws and regulations and therefore free for general use.

The publisher, the authors and the editors are safe to assume that the advice and information in this book are believed to be true and accurate at the date of publication. Neither the publisher nor the authors or the editors give a warranty, expressed or implied, with respect to the material contained herein or for any errors or omissions that may have been made. The publisher remains neutral with regard to jurisdictional claims in published maps and institutional affiliations.

Cover illustration: © Melisa Hasan

This Palgrave Macmillan imprint is published by the registered company Springer Nature Switzerland AG
The registered company address is: Gewerbestrasse 11, 6330 Cham, Switzerland

Paper in this product is recyclable.

*For my wife Yordanos and daughters Penelope and Sienna, whose birth coincided with the publication of this book*
—*Alex Urmeneta*

*For my daughter Cyan, my husband and family, who has supported me through my academic journey*
—*Margarida Romero*

# Acknowledgements

This book is a testament to the power of collaboration, drawing on the expertise of international and multidisciplinary researchers. The diverse backgrounds and experiences displayed reflect our concerted effort to bring much needed context to the existing research around AI in education. The editors would like to acknowledge the contributions and research of all the participating authors and extend our sincere gratitude for entrusting us with their work. We would also like to thank the learners whose voices and viewpoints we have strived to highlight and amplify. Finally, our thanks to the universities, research groups, companies and educational institutions with which the authors are affiliated, all of whom have been instrumental in the realisation of this project.

| | |
|---|---|
| Thenon, France | Alex Urmeneta |
| Nice, France | Margarida Romero |
| January 2024 | |

# Contents

**Part I  Creative Applications of Artificial Intelligence in Education**

1 Creative Application of Artificial Intelligence in Education    3
   *Alex Urmeneta and Margarida Romero*

2 Preserving Teacher and Student Agency: Insights from a Literature Review    17
   *Alexandre Lepage and Simon Collin*

3 Learning Artificial Intelligence Through Open Educational Resources    35
   *Frédéric Alexandre, Marie-Helene Comte, Aurélie Lagarrigue, and Thierry Viéville*

4 Digital Acculturation in the Era of Artificial Intelligence    45
   *Michel Durampart, Philippe Bonfils, and Margarida Romero*

5   Citizenship, Censorship, and Democracy in the Age
    of Artificial Intelligence   57
    *Tetiana Matusevych, Margarida Romero,
    and Oksana Strutynska*

Part II   Artificial Intelligence in K-12 Education

6   International Initiatives and Regional Ecosystems
    for Supporting Artificial Intelligence Acculturation   75
    *Margarida Romero, Isabelle Galy, Jérémy Camponovo,
    Florence Tressols, and Alex Urmeneta*

7   Informal Education Practices for Human–AI Creative
    Pedagogy for Accessibility and Inclusivity   89
    *Caroline Boulord, Yann-Aël Le Borgne, and Patricia Corieri*

8   Students' Perspective on the Use of Artificial
    Intelligence in Education   101
    *Christelle Caucheteux, Lianne-Blue Hodgkins,
    Victoire Batifol, Laurent Fouché, and Margarida Romero*

Part III   Artificial Intelligence in Higher Education

9   Affordances for AI-Enhanced Digital Game-Based
    Learning   117
    *Margarida Romero, Petros Lameras, and Sylvester Arnab*

10  Generative Artificial Intelligence in Higher Education   129
    *Margarida Romero, Jonathan Reyes, and Panos Kostakos*

11  Artificial Intelligence in Professional and Vocational
    Training   145
    *Solange Ciavaldini-Cartaut, Jean-François Métral,
    Paul Olry, Dominique Guidoni-Stoltz,
    and Charles-Antoine Gagneur*

12 **Manifesto in Defence of Human-Centred Education
in the Age of Artificial Intelligence** 157
*Margarida Romero, Thomas Frosig,
Amanda M. L. Taylor-Beswick, Jari Laru,
Bastienne Bernasco, Alex Urmeneta, Oksana Strutynska,
and Marc-André Girard*

**Index** 179

# Notes on Contributors

**Frédéric Alexandre** is an Inria Director of Research, head of the Mnemosyne team affiliated to Inria, CNRS, Université de Bordeaux, Bordeaux INP, through UMR LaBRI and IMN. The team aims at developing systemic models of the brain using formalism of computational neuroscience and is specifically interested in understanding how high-level cognitive functions emerge from the synergy between different kinds of memory. The team is hosted on the Bordeaux hospital campus, favouring medical and neurobiological applications, but investigations in machine learning and artificial intelligence are also considered.

**Sylvester Arnab** is a Professor in Game Science (Applied Games) at Coventry University, where he is leading the Ludic Design research group. His research focuses on how engaging, immersive and empowering experiences are designed and applied based on strategies and elements commonly used by playful and game-based approaches (analogue and/or digital) and how their operations are underpinned by pedagogical and motivational theories and practices. Sylvester co-founded the multi-award-winning GameChangers initiative (https://gchangers.org).

**Victoire Batifol** teacher of French at Life Bloom Academy and in different highschools like Lycée Renoir, has studied at Université Jean Monnet Saint-Étienne. Her influence extends beyond the classroom, making her an integral part of the Life Bloom community, where she imparts knowledge and ignites a love for the French language.

**Bastienne Bernasco** is a Senior Lecturer and researcher at the Hospitality Business School at Saxion University of Applied Sciences in the Netherlands. She is Green Ambassador at Saxion and specialises in learning sciences, sustainability, and the ethics of technology. She lectures in responsible leadership, sustainability and ethics of technology. She enjoys coaching interdisciplinary student teams working on wicked societal issues such as sustainable water management and building sustainable local food systems.

**Philippe Bonfils** Professor of Information and Communication Sciences at the University of Toulon and member of the Institut Méditerranéen des Sciences de l'Information et de la Communication (IMSIC), coordinates various research projects on the analysis of new forms and changes in communication and mediation processes at work in socio-technical learning devices such as immersive environments. He is now involved in several generative IA research projects.

**Caroline Boulord** is a Ph.D. in Physics and the Project Administrator and Organizer at La Scientothèque ASBL. Her work revolves around managing and coordinating various projects for La Scientothèque, an association committed to promoting science, technology, engineering, arts, and mathematics (STEAM) education. With a passion for education and outreach, Caroline actively contributes to organising workshops, events, and educational initiatives that aim to make science and technology accessible to diverse audiences.

**Jérémy Camponovo** currently serving as a Project Manager at the DANE (Academic Delegation for Digital Education) in Nice, is also a physics, chemistry and computer science teacher at the International College of Valbonne. Dedicated to fostering digital education, he actively involves his students in computer learning activities and extends his impact by training fellow educators in his role as a project manager at the DANE.

**Christelle Caucheteux** is the Founder and Pedagogical Coordinator of Life Bloom Academy, a middle school dedicated to nurturing young minds. Her passion for education is evident in her role as a history and geography teacher, where she goes beyond conventional methods, engaging teenagers in transformative co-creative pedagogical projects. Notable initiatives include "Apprentis Entrepreneurs," a programme fostering entrepreneurial skills, and "Find your Ikigai," an enriching series of out-of-school and summer camp activities.

**Solange Ciavaldini-Cartaut** is Professor of Educational Sciences at the Université Côte d'Azur in France. Her field of research concerns learning and development processes in educational and training environments and health issues in work contexts. Therefore, her research framework is based on activity theories, professional didactics, and social psychology. Her actual research focuses on school wellbeing, pedagogical design, and innovation for adult education and skills development.

**Simon Collin** is a Professor in the Faculty of Education at the Université du Québec à Montréal (UQÀM). He holds the Canada Research Chair on Digital Equity in Education and is a researcher at the Interuniversity Research Center on Teacher Training and Teaching (CRIFPE). His academic background and research interests focus on the issues of digital equity in education, which he addresses by combining interdisciplinary studies on technology and critical approaches.

**Marie-Helene Comte** is a Pedagogical Engineer with a focus on advancing educational initiatives through digital platforms. Since late 2013, she has been a key contributor at Inria Learning Lab, where she coordinates the development of Massive Open Online Courses (MOOCs) and oversees pedagogical engineering. Engaged in scientific mediation and actively participating in a committee dedicated to reflecting on digital education, she collaborates with educators and researchers to shape the future of online teaching.

**Patricia Corieri** Director at La Scientothèque ASBL, spearheads STEAM education initiatives. Committed to reducing inequalities, she contributes to social cohesion programmes, Erasmus+ projects (e.g. Steamcity), and manages ESERO ESA's educational programme for the French and German community of Belgium. With a Ph.D. in Fluid Dynamics and degrees in pedagogy, Patricia's dedication to science education aligns with La Scientothèque's mission, ensuring equal opportunities through innovative educational programmes.

**Michel Durampart** is a Full Professor and member of the council of the SHS doctoral school (ED 509) of the University of Toulon and the College of Doctoral Schools. He has been Director of the IMSIC UTLN-AMU laboratory in information and communication sciences (Universities of Toulon and Aix-Marseille) since 2017. He conducts research at the national and international levels on the relationships and complementarities between knowledge and societies linked to digital devices and digital communication, as well as the evolution of learning and cognitive issues in relation to digital devices and tools.

**Laurent Fouché** STEAM Professor at Life Bloom Academy, champions interdisciplinary research. With a dedicated focus on Science, Technology, Engineering and Mathematics, he inspires a holistic approach to education. Laurent's commitment to fostering cross-disciplinary connections enhances the academic experience for students, creating a dynamic and enriching learning environment.

**Thomas Frosig** started with EdTech in 2006, developing the first 3D multiplayer game for the Danish Department of Education, while also working with LEGO Education. Moving to Germany in 2016, he started consulting for various departments of education, leading teacher training in the creative use of EdTech in classrooms. He holds an MSc in Educational Technology from the smartEdTech programme at Université Côte d'Azur. Currently he's a Senior digital content developer in the global excellence and training team at Leschaco GmbH, while also pursuing his Ph.D. in the cross-disciplinary fields of learning sciences, cognitive neuroscience, and game-based learning.

**Dr. Charles-Antoine Gagneur** is Associate Researcher at the University of Burgundy, specialising in vocational education. His research explores reflective expertise and organisation redesign, contributing to professional training. His actual work bridges his roles as an independent consultant, digital platform designer, and researcher to design learning environments for adult education and skills development.

**Isabelle Galy** is the Director General of the Maison de l'Intelligence Artificielle (MIA), bringing a wealth of diverse experience with a consistent focus on innovative technologies and their resulting ecosystems. With a decade-long commitment at Club Sénat, she has worked to create a conducive environment for digital advancement. Currently, Isabelle sustains these efforts through her commitment to AI ecosystems as the Vice-President of ClusterIA, Board advisor @RaisinAI, Founder member of Hub France IA, board member of #JamaisSansElles, and French ambassador at the Women 20. Her dedication to fostering technological innovation and impactful digital ecosystems underscores her role as a dynamic leader at the forefront of AI intelligence initiatives.

**Marc-André Girard** is an experienced school director, integrating practical experience in school leadership with extensive research. He recently earned a Professional Doctorate in Education (2022) from Sherbrooke University, in Canada. Specializing in school change management and pedagogical transformation, he serves as a school principal and engages as a speaker on topics such as educational leadership, digital pedagogical approaches, and school change. As the author of a trilogy on the twenty-first-century school (2019), he actively contributes to educational discourse and was honoured with the 2016 AQUOPS CHAPO prize.

**Dominique Guidoni-Stoltz** is an Associate Researcher in the Formation et Apprentissages Professionnels research unit (FoAP) at the Institut-Agro Dijon. Her field of research is vocational didactics: the analysis of work and learning for vocational training. Her current research focuses on the analysis of forestry work, training, and learning, with a view to designing a pedagogical simulator for forestry learning (SilvaNumerica).

**Lianne-Blue Hodgkins** English Teacher at Life Bloom Academy middle school, manages classes of multiple skill levels from beginner to native, hitting learning goals, and managing parent–teacher relations. Her mission involves creating and managing a number of pedagogical projects including termly newsletters, curriculum-based board games and workshop activities, theatre performances, and curriculum-based cross subject projects.

**Panos Kostakos** is a Senior Research Fellow at the Center for Ubiquitous Computing, University of Oulu, Finland, and Chief Researcher at Kaunas University of Technology, Lithuania. His research is situated at the intersection of Artificial Intelligence, Information Security and Security orchestration, focusing on autonomous, mutable, and cognitive cyber defence mechanisms. He leads the Cyber Security Informatics (CSI) research group.

**Aurélie Lagarrigue** is employed at Inria Learning Lab as a Pedagogical Engineer, where she contributes to the development of multiple Massive Open Online Courses (MOOCs) utilising digital technologies. Her primary objective is to promote digital literacy and enlighten the public on a variety of topics.

**Petros Lameras** is an Associate Professor in Digital Media at the Centre of Post-Digital Cultures, Coventry University, UK. His research focuses on the intersection of AI, games and education, with a particular emphasis on empowering educators to leverage immersive technologies in the creation and orchestration of effective learning resources. With a robust background in computer science ranging from games technology and interactive media to mobile application development and multimodal interface design, Petros has contributed significantly to national and international research projects in technology-enhanced learning, specifically in the realm of STEM education. His research contributions are well-documented in digital learning conferences and high-impact publications, shedding light on the transformative role of games and AI in education.

**Jari Laru** is a Ph.D. in Education, University Lecturer in Technology Enhanced Learning at the Faculty of Education & Psychology, University of Oulu, Finland. His research focuses on the intersection of learning sciences and emerging technologies. He has done his doctoral thesis in the context of mobile learning and currently is working on the Generation AI project funded by the Strategic Research Council, Finland.

**Yann-Aël Le Borgne** is a Ph.D. in Computer Science, AI expert for La Scientothèque ASBL, and scientific collaborator at the Machine Learning Group—Université Libre de Bruxelles, Belgium. His research interests include machine learning and big data technologies, with a focus on applications related to IoT and environmental monitoring. Within La Scientothèque, he contributes to the design of STEAM and AI activities for K-12.

**Alexandre Lepage** holds a Master's degree in educational technology from the Université Laval, Canada, and is pursuing a Ph.D. at the Université de Montréal. He teaches various courses about ICT in education, artificial intelligence in education and instructional design. His thesis focuses on the adoption of artificial intelligence by higher education teachers. He has worked as an instructional designer and digital education specialist for Quebec's Ministry of Education.

**Tetiana Matusevych** is a Ph.D. in Philosophy of Education, Associate Professor at UNESCO Chair on Science Education, Dragomanov Ukrainian State University, Ukraine, and collaborator at the Institute of Gender Studies, Carlos III University of Madrid, Spain. Her research focuses on developing responsible citizenship through science education, the socio-cultural dimension of AI in education, and gender equality policies and practices in education.

**Jean-François Métral** is in charge of research and training in Education and Training Sciences at the Institut-Agro Dijon. His research focuses on the development of professional skills in training and at work, and draws on activity theories from a vocational didactics perspective.

**Paul Olry** is Professor Emeritus at the University of Burgundy, Institut-Agro. His field of research concerns learning at work in professional sectors where skills are at stake. This is why his work draws on the theories of activity, professional didactics, and transmission. His research focuses on the analysis of work that is difficult to see, its formalisation, and the design of formats and resources for learning.

**Jonathan Reyes** holds a Master's in educational technologies and is a Pedagogical Engineer and EdTech innovator at Université Côte d'Azur. His contributions to numerous international projects have led to the creation of programmes for various fields of knowledge including empowering HEI professors in chatbot creation, artificial intelligence, and digital soft skills.

**Margarida Romero** is a Full Professor at Université Côte d'Azur in France and an Associate Professor at Université Laval in Canada. After starting her career at the Universitat Autonoma de Barcelona where she was awarded the best doctoral thesis in psychology, she continued her career in Canada and France, where she set up the Laboratoire d'Innovation et Numérique pour l'Education (LINE), a research unit in the learning sciences. She coordinates the #Scol_IA Working Group on the educational challenges of artificial intelligence in education and co-directs the international MSc SmartEdTech programme.

**Oksana Strutynska** is a Full Professor at Dragomanov Ukrainian State University (Kyiv, Ukraine) and researcher in LINE lab, University Cote D'Azur (Nice, France). She is academic coordinator of the STREAM project (under Erasmus+ Jean Monnet Module since 2022). She has set up the new BSc and MSc programme for preparing pre-service Computer Science Teachers to teach Educational Robotics (since 2018). Her main research and academic interests focus on Educational Robotics, 3D technology and AI in education.

**Professor Amanda M. L. Taylor-Beswick** is the Director of Digital Transformation at the University of Cumbria, England, UK. She is also a social scientist with an interest in the socio-technological intersection of the future of work and education, with a particular emphasis on the digitalisation of professional and higher education. An award-winning and published academic, she is recognised for leading critical and ethical discourse in digitalisation, and the development of pedagogic approaches that support the progression of information and media literacies for academics, students and practitioners already practising in their respective fields. Amanda is an impactful educator leading transformational digital policy and practice change within a range of professional groupings. She is also a qualified social worker by professional background, with extensive practice experience in psychiatric social work and work with d/deaf children and families.

**Dr. Florence Tressols** is a consultant in wellbeing for business and educational actors, who forged her path after a career as a Senior Business Architect in digital technologies, artificial intelligence and societal impacts. With a background encompassing roles at prominent entities such as IBM and the Maison de l'Intelligence Artificielle, she combines her expertise in digital technologies with a societal commitment to supporting youth and professionals to thrive through different challenges.

**Alex Urmeneta** is a Learning Experience Strategist specialising in the development of innovative curricula and content within startup environments. His focus is on creating impactful educational content by fusing the latest pedagogical strategies with cutting-edge technology. Prior to his work in education, Alex held leadership roles in the finance and technology sectors, both in the United States as well as internationally. He holds an MSc in Education Technology from the Université Côte d' Azur in France as well as an MEd from Arizona State University.

**Thierry Viéville** is a Senior Researcher at the National Research Institute in Computer Science and Control Theory (Inria) where he works in Computational Neurosciences with the Mnemosyne research team and in the LINE laboratory focusing on education in computer science. He is a Bio-Medical Engineer from the Ecole Nationale Superieure des Telecommunications (Bretagne and Paris), with a Master's in Mathematics, a Master's, a Ph.D. in Neuro-Science, and the Habilitation to Conduct Researches (HDR) in Engineering-Science.

# List of Figures

| | | |
|---|---|---|
| Fig. 1.1 | Creative engagement in AI in education | 8 |
| Fig. 1.2 | Organisation of the chapters in three parts | 11 |
| Fig. 1.3 | AI application in educational settings | 13 |
| Fig. 3.1 | An example of an unplugged activity for experimenting with a reinforcement learning algorithm | 41 |
| Fig. 6.1 | World AI Cannes Festival | 85 |
| Fig. 12.1 | Six levels of creative engagement in human–AI in education | 169 |

# Part I

## Creative Applications of Artificial Intelligence in Education

# 1

# Creative Application of Artificial Intelligence in Education

Alex Urmeneta and Margarida Romero

**Abstract** The chapter commences by presenting the emergence of artificial intelligence (AI) in the field of education. It aims to provide an overview of the AI environment in education, highlighting the importance of a nuanced comprehension of its effects, ethical implications, and potential to stimulate innovative teaching methods. The chapter explores the historical background of technological interventions in education and takes a critical approach to examining the potential benefits and drawbacks of AI. It also considers the sociocultural and creative aspects of using AI in education. AI has typically focused on imitating human intelligence. Within the realm of human abilities, we recognise various degrees of creative involvement in AI in education, which demonstrates its capacity to revolutionise learning experiences. At the most advanced

---

A. Urmeneta (✉) · M. Romero
Université Côte d'Azur, Nice, France
e-mail: alex.urmeneta@etu.univ-cotedazur.fr

M. Romero
e-mail: margarida.romero@univ-cotedazur.fr; margarida.romero@unice.fr

---

© The Author(s) 2024
A. Urmeneta and M. Romero (eds.), *Creative Applications of Artificial Intelligence in Education*, Palgrave Studies in Creativity and Culture,
https://doi.org/10.1007/978-3-031-55272-4_1

stages of creative involvement, we explore the possibilities for collaboration between human intelligence and AI, suggesting a viewpoint of human–AI co-creativity. The chapter also outlines the book's structure, which consists of three main sections: the creative engagement approach, real examples in K-12 education, and advances and prospects in higher education. The different chapters envision not only the acculturation and education of AI, but also the potential of human–AI collaboration to support learners in expressing their unique talents and developing expansive, AI-supported learning initiatives.

**Keywords** Creativity · AI education · Artificial intelligence · Hybrid intelligence · Human–AI collaboration · K-12 education · AI ethics · Creative pedagogies

## Introduction

The recent availability of Artificial Intelligence (AI) applications has increased public interest and sparked curiosity about the potential of Large Language Models (LLMs) and other forms of generative AI. These models, enabled by parallel breakthroughs in data management, cloud computing, and artificial neural networks (Zhai et al., 2021), are viewed by some as the catalyst for the fourth industrial revolution (Bühler et al., 2022). One might wonder what the scholars who first used the term "Artificial Intelligence" in the late 1950s would think of its nearly 70-year journey to our current understanding and definitions of AI. Their definition of AI as "the science and engineering of making intelligent machines" seems modest given where we are today—still seemingly at the dawn of AI's potential. Perhaps this is why there has been much debate in recent years about what constitutes AI, as different stakeholders seek to assign meaning that aligns with their own needs and goals (Samoili et al., 2020). It is through this lens that educational stakeholders are now considering the role of AI in education as they seek to define its use cases, impact, and potential challenges going forward.

Education, ever ripe for change in response to current educational and societal challenges, has been earmarked as one of the domains in which the benefits of AI can be developed, but also an area that necessitates adherence to rigorous ethical principles. It is crucial for technology to prioritise the protection of privacy and the well-being of students and their communities. The study of the potential of AI for education opens many different perspectives that need to be considered within the context of Technology Enhanced Learning (TEL) and its evolution in recent decades. This stands to reason given the complex role technology has played over the years in creating expectations around its ability to support the teaching and learning process. From headphones to projectors to calculators and personal computers, the internet, smart devices, and MOOCs, each iteration carried with it a level of optimism and promise that this would be the technological advancement that transformed education for the better (Escueta et al., 2017, Higgins et al., 2012, Zhai et al., 2021). Nevertheless, such optimism warrants scrutiny when viewed through the lens of techno-solutionism (Selwyn, 2022), a perspective that emphasises a critical examination of technology's role and its limitations in solving complex societal issues such the Sustainable Development Goals (SDGs). While technological advancements have improved some processes and supported the creation of others, the techno-solutionism perspective (Elfert, 2023). Urges us to question the effectiveness of these innovations and whether they genuinely address root challenges or merely present a valueless transformation of the teaching and learning process. This sociocritical perspective in TEL encourages a nuanced understanding of the relationship between technology and education, prompting us to assess not only the potential benefits but also the unintended consequences and limitations associated with each wave of technological adoption (Collin & Brotcorne, 2019). In doing so, we can cultivate a more informed and balanced approach to leveraging technology for educational advancement. Yet, with use cases frequently driven by commercial interests or entities employing opaque development principles, many of these advancements have had, arguably, mixed results when it comes to transforming the learning experience or the prevailing pedagogy of the time. Certainly, the inclusion of personal computers, smart devices, and internet access in educational settings has felt important for a great number of students and educators, but to say that these technologies have radically altered how the majority of students learn may well be looked upon decades from now as recency bias (Zhai et al., 2021). Rather, it might be more accurate to say that technology has served as a catalyst of sorts pushing stakeholders in the developed world to reconsider some teaching and learning processes, even while lacking the capacity required to fundamentally improve said processes. For example, while videoconference technologies have supported the rise of remote learning, the underlying teaching and learning experience remains largely uneven and, in some cases, has actually given rise to a host of new challenges requiring their own technological and pedagogical solutions. We see this in studies developed during the pandemic, where the issue of videoconference fatigue (Bennett et al., 2021) and technostress (Anh et al., 2023) were identified in both students and educators. Yet, even through this historical lens, the current levels of both promise and concern being afforded to AI and AI tools seems magnitudes greater than the introduction of earlier education technologies. In fact, Seldon et al. (2020) views AI as the Fourth Education Revolution considering a context in which AI is recognised by different authors as a lever of the Fourth Industrial Revolution (4IR). It is our hope that this book goes some way towards explaining how AI could serve as a powerful force for change within education, but more specifically, as a collaborative tool furthering the cause of human–AI creativity.

## From Human Intelligence Emulation to Human–AI Creativity

The current hype surrounding AI may seem sudden, but in fact researchers have been building towards this moment since the 1950s. AI used to be the purview of researchers and science fiction authors living firmly in the realm of imagination. AI encompasses the emulation of human intelligence by machines or computer systems. It involves the development of algorithms and computational models that enable machines to perform tasks typically associated with human cognition, such as problem-solving, learning, and decision-making (Ng et al., 2023). AI systems leverage data and advanced algorithms to analyse patterns, draw insights, and adapt their behaviour over time, aiming to replicate and augment human-like intelligence. This evolving field encompasses various subfields, including machine learning, natural language processing, and computer vision, contributing to the continuous refinement and expansion of AI capabilities. The ubiquitousness of generative AI tools and their ease of use has significantly altered the public perception around their usefulness. In recent years, a major disruption has emerged with the rise of generative AI and the availability of technologies such as Chat GPT, Midjourney, and AI chatbots and their relative ease of use. Today, AI can be found in any number of applications serving a diverse number of sectors and uses. From writing assistants to x-ray diagnostic tools to data processing, a significant percentage of the population has reportedly experimented with AI tools (Chui et al., 2023). Despite the current enthusiasm, there remains a considerable amount of work to be done around the risks associated with these tools. Questions of access, bias, data protection and privacy, use of copyrighted material in training models, and responsible use are growing louder as stakeholders struggle to keep pace with the rapid growth of AI use.

The traditional definitions of AI encompass a simulation paradigm in which artificial systems aim to replicate human systems. However, this approach does not consider its potential not only as human-like intelligence but as a cooperation tool for human–AI collaboration. Creativity is a complex human phenomenon that researchers try to replicate through artificial creativity systems. In education, considering creative pedagogy as a paradigm presents its own challenges given that there are no set methods explaining how to be creative; rather, strategies that facilitate the creative process (Pinillos & Vallverdú, 2021). This is supported by cognitive research showing creativity not as a construct of some novel process within the brain, but rather a combination of executive functions, neurochemical reactions and other mental processes (Beaty et al., 2018; Boccia et al., 2015). Given the lack of concrete instruction on how to be creative, how then should we consider the process of human creativity in relation to AI systems and associated concepts such as computational creativity?

For the international group of researchers contributing to this book, the answer lies in viewing the efforts of both systems as co-contributors with the shared goal of facilitating creativity—both as a function of process as well as ideation. As AI systems have become more prevalent and accessible, the relationship between humans and AI has evolved beyond process automation to a more collaborative partnership based on shared synergies and strengths (Razmerita et al., 2022) and the metacognitive potential of human–AI collaboration (Romero et al., 2023). It is at this intersection between human intuition and imagination and AI's computation power and processing capabilities where we see the greatest potential for human–AI co-creativity. In fact, we can already see this potential today across a number of creative domains including music composition and performance (Rohrmeier, 2022) and in the visual arts where artists have leveraged AI tools to expand their creative process (Kim et al., 2021) through an extensive learning approach where AI serves transformational objectives (Romero et al., 2023). For our purposes though, it is the potential for revisiting creativity through the lens of human–AI interactions, innovative teaching strategies, and learner-centric activities that could support learners' agency and a creative pedagogy supported by human–AI activities.

For facilitating the identification of the different levels of creative engagement in the use of AI, the Passive-Participatory (PP) model for AI in education (#PPai6) distinguishes six levels of creative engagement (Fig. 1.1).

At the first level, learners act as passive consumers, engaging with AI-generated content without a full understanding of its workings. Moving

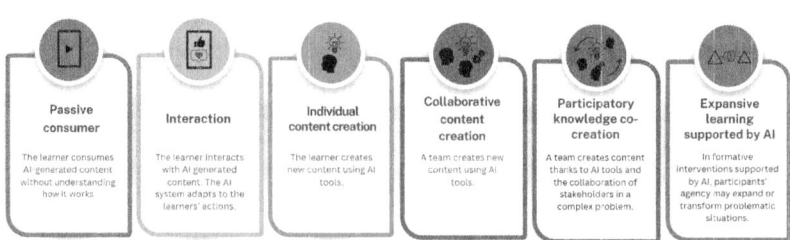

Fig. 1.1 Creative engagement in AI in education

through the levels, learners progress to become interactive consumers, actively interacting with AI-generated content as the AI system adapts to their actions. Levels three and four involve individual and collaborative content creation, respectively, with learners utilising AI tools to generate new content. The fifth level, participatory knowledge co-creation, sees teams creating content with the aid of AI tools and collaboration from stakeholders to tackle complex problems. At the sixth and most advanced level, expansive learning supported by AI, participants' agency expands or transforms problematic situations through formative interventions. AI tools play a crucial role in identifying contradictions in complex problems, generating concepts or artefacts to regulate conflicting stimuli, and fostering collective agency and action. While the potential for AI to reach this transformative level is immense, it is noteworthy that the majority of current AI in education studies operate at the second level (interactive consumer), primarily relying on Intelligent Tutoring Systems (ITS). The exploration of higher levels presents an exciting frontier for the future development and implementation of AI in education that will be explored through the different case studies of this book.

## AI in Education, a Critical Domain for the Society

AI has emerged as a disruptive technology that holds the capacity to revolutionise certain educational endeavours, such as the composition of written essays or the facilitation of hybrid intelligence approaches (Järvelä et al., 2023; Molenaar, 2022). These hybrid systems, which amalgamate artificial and human intelligence, have the potential to enhance the pedagogical process by providing support for teaching and learning activities. AI, as a disruptive technology, possesses the capacity to revolutionise the process of knowledge creation for various educational stakeholders, including students, faculty members, and society as a whole. AI possesses the potential to not only be incorporated into hybrid systems designed to foster learners' agency and creativity, but also to facilitate the personalisation of the learning process. Through the utilisation of sophisticated algorithms and extensive datasets, AI possesses the capability to facilitate the adaptability of digital educational environments, including educational serious games (Zhan et al., 2022). The primary objective of the individualised approach is to facilitate the active involvement of learners and offer tailored feedback that is contingent upon the specific nature of the learning tasks at hand. Though the use of learning analytics, AI technologies have the capability to facilitate the automation of administrative tasks, as well as detect and analyse potential challenges encountered by learners in their digital educational journeys.

Within the context of AI in education, much of the research has centred around institutional or strategic applications and AI in the practice of teaching and learning (Bates et al., 2020). Institutional applications primarily deal with data mining or AI's ability to organise huge data sets into relevant outcomes. This is particularly useful for helping educational institutions identify and diagnose systemic and individual problems within the current education framework (Zhai et al., 2021). The second approach, and the primary focus of this book, is how AI can enhance the learning experience by redefining current teaching strategies, expanding pathways for learning, and reducing or eliminating barriers to knowledge transfer. Specifically, the book explores the dynamic intersection of AI, education, and creativity, focusing on how human–AI learning activities can unleash creative pedagogies (Leroy & Romero, 2021; Lin, 2011; Selkrig & Keamy, 2017).

Education is not merely about imparting knowledge; it is about nurturing creative thinking, fostering critical skills, and empowering individuals to become lifelong learners. With the rapid advancement of AI, we are on the brink of a new era where intelligent technologies can enhance the learning experience in unprecedented ways, not only in relation to the personalisation of learning activities but to human–AI collaborations where AI supports the creative process of learners and teachers. In this context, we have the opportunity to redefine the boundaries of creative pedagogies by integrating AI into pedagogical practices at different educational levels and domains, thereby creating new opportunities for engaging, personalised, and transformative learning experiences through an expansive learning approach (Engeström & Sannino, 2021; Romero et al., 2023).

Through this book we aim not only to address the current practices of AI in education but also to develop further the opportunities and potentialities of co-creativity in human–AI technologies. The next section will introduce the organisation of the book towards these two main objectives.

## The Organisation of the Book

This book focuses on the concept of creative application of AI in education as its central theme to address the pedagogical strategies for integrating AI in different educational settings ranging from primary to higher education, but also in outreach and citizen AI literacy activities. As such, the book is structured in three parts (Fig. 1.2).

1. The first part begins to develop the creative engagement perspective for learning and teaching AI, while describing how to use AI in creative ways through an expansive learning approach.
2. The second part of the book focuses on concrete examples of AI in K-12 education, not only from a researcher and teacher's perspective, but giving learners the possibility to define their own vision, perspective,

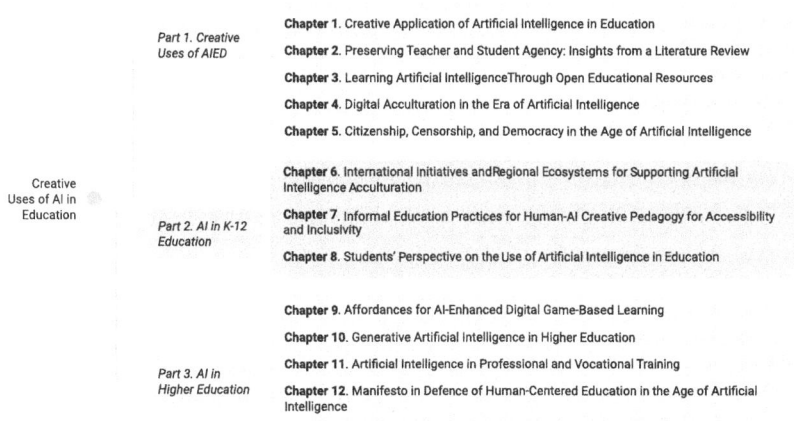

Fig. 1.2 Organisation of the chapters in three parts

doubts and worries related to the introduction of AI in education. These perspectives are important given that these learners will have a significant impact on our future society based on their relationships with these intelligent tools, established during their formative school years, and refined through their professional careers.
3. The third part of the book is devoted to the advances and opportunities of AI in higher education, covering not only different fields (e.g. teacher education, professional education, business education) but also different types of AI-supported tools such as games, chatbots, and AI assisted assessment.

Through these different activities, we propose concrete examples of how education could benefit from empowering all educational stakeholders in their AI literacy and their capacity to design human–AI learning activities that foster creativity, inspire critical thinking, and promote problem-solving by embracing AI as a tool for expansive learning.

The book also investigates the application of AI in various educational settings. From intelligent tutoring systems to adaptive game-based learning platforms, and from large language models such as ChatGPT to adaptive computer-supported collaborative learning (CSCL), we set out to analyse the various domains wherein AI can have a significant impact on enhancing the learning experience. Additionally, we examine how AI technologies can be integrated into both formal and informal education to empower educators, learners, and their communities, supporting co-creative human–AI activities and the development of transformative agency (Fig. 1.3).

The book "Creative Applications of Artificial Intelligence in Education" is both a roadmap and a catalyst for further exploration into human–AI co-creativity. It is a snapshot of our current position at the dawn of AI and educational synergies, but is also intended to encourage more multidisciplinary discussions around the benefits and potential challenges learners and educators face as we integrate and evolve this new relationship as co-creators. Join us then on this exciting and transformative journey as we investigate creative pedagogies and explore the integration of AI in education. Together, let's develop and cultivate

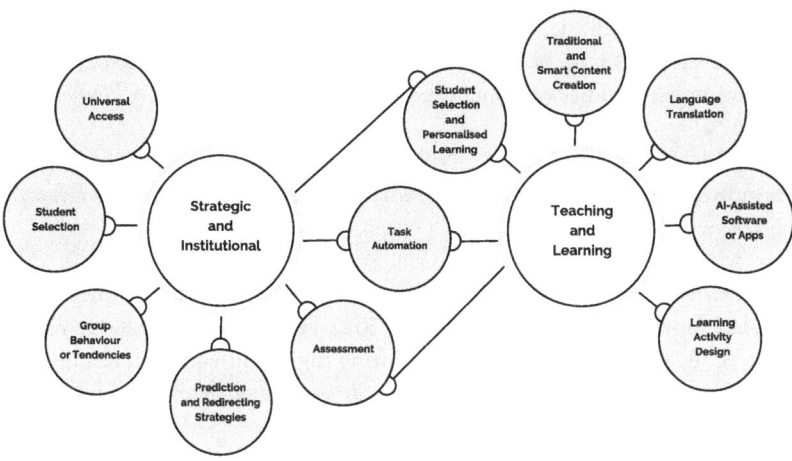

**Fig. 1.3** AI application in educational settings

multiple perspectives on the impact of AI in education, harness its potential, and consider scenarios where human–AI collaboration can support learners seeking to creatively express their unique talents and develop expansive AI-supported learning initiatives.

## References

Anh, L. T., Whelan, E., & Umair, A. (2023). 'You're still on mute'. A study of video conferencing fatigue during the COVID-19 pandemic from a technostress perspective. *Behaviour & Information Technology, 42*(11), 1758–1772.

Beaty, R. E., Thakral, P. P., Madore, K. P., Benedek, M., & Schacter, D. L. (2018). Core network contributions to remembering the past, imagining the future, and thinking creatively. *Journal of Cognitive Neuroscience, 30*(12), 1939–1951.

Bennett, A. A., Campion, E. D., Keeler, K. R., & Keener, S. K. (2021). Videoconference fatigue? Exploring changes in fatigue after videoconference meetings during COVID-19. *Journal of Applied Psychology, 106*(3), 330.

Boccia, M., Piccardi, L., Palermo, L., Nori, R., & Palmiero, M. (2015). Where do bright ideas occur in our brain? Meta-analytic evidence from neuroimaging studies of domainspecific creativity. *Frontiers in Psychology, 6*, 155624.

Bühler, M. M., Jelinek, T., & Nübel, K. (2022). Training and preparing tomorrow's workforce for the fourth industrial revolution. *Education Sciences, 12*(11), 782.

Chui, M., Yee, L., Hall, B., & Singla, A. (2023). *The state of AI in 2023: Generative AI's breakout year*. https://www.mckinsey.com/capabilities/quantumblack/our-insights/the-state-of-ai-in-2023-generative-ais-breakout-year

Collin, S., & Brotcorne, P. (2019). Capturing digital (in)equity in teaching and learning: A sociocritical approach. *The International Journal of Information and Learning Technology, 36*(2), 169–180.

Elfert, M. (2023). Humanism and democracy in comparative education. *Comparative Education, 59*(3), 1–18.

Engeström, Y., & Sannino, A. (2021). From mediated actions to heterogenous coalitions: Four generations of activity-theoretical studies of work and learning. *Mind, Culture, and Activity, 28*(1), 4–23.

Escueta, M., Quan, V., Nickow, A. J., & Oreopoulos, P. (2017). *Education technology: An evidence-based review* (Working Paper 23744). National Bureau of Economic Research. https://doi.org/10.3386/w23744

Higgins, S., Xiao, Z., & Katsipataki, M. (2012). *The impact of digital technology on learning: A summary for the Education Endowment Foundation*. Full Report. Education Endowment Foundation. https://eric.ed.gov/?id=ED612174

Järvelä, S., Nguyen, A., & Hadwin, A. (2023). Human and artificial intelligence collaboration for socially shared regulation in learning. *British Journal of Educational Technology, 54*(2), 1057–1076.

Kim, S. L., Cheong, M., Srivastava, A., Yoo, Y., & Yun, S. (2021). Knowledge sharing and creative behavior: The interaction effects of knowledge sharing and regulatory focus on creative behavior. *Human Performance, 34*(1), 49–66.

Leroy, A., & Romero, M. (2021). Teachers' creative behaviors in STEAM Activities with modular robotics. In *Frontiers in Education* (Vol. 6, p. 642147).

Lin, Y. S. (2011). Fostering creativity through education–a conceptual framework of creative pedagogy. *Creative education, 2*(03), 149.

Molenaar, I. (2022). The concept of hybrid human-AI regulation: Exemplifying how to support young learners' self-regulated learning. *Computers and Education: Artificial Intelligence, 3*, 100070.

Ng, D. T. K., Lee, M., Tan, R. J. Y., Hu, X., Downie, J. S., & Chu, S. K. W. (2023). A review of AI teaching and learning from 2000 to 2020. *Education and Information Technologies, 28*(7), 8445–8501.

Pinillos, A. S., & Vallverdú, J. (2021). What the#®¥ § ≠ $@ is Creativity?. *Debats. Revista de cultura, poder i societat*, 135–147.

Razmerita, L., Brun, A., & Nabeth, T. (2022). Collaboration in the machine age: Trustworthy human-AI collaboration. In *Advances in Selected Artificial Intelligence Areas: World Outstanding Women in Artificial Intelligence* (pp. 333–356). Cham: Springer International Publishing.

Rohrmeier, M. (2022). On creativity, music's AI completeness, and four challenges for artificial musical creativity. *Trans. Int. Soc. Music. Inf. Retr., 5*(1), 50–66.

Romero, M., Heiser, L., Lepage, A., Gagnebien, A., Bonjour, A., Lagarrigue, A., ... & Borgne, Y. A. L. (2023). *Teaching and learning in the age of artificial intelligence.* arXiv preprint arXiv:2303.06956.

Samoili, S., Cobo, M. L., Gomez, E., De Prato, G., Martinez-Plumed, F., & Delipetrev, B. (2020). *AI watch. Defining artificial intelligence. Towards an operational definition and taxonomy of artificial intelligence* (No. JRC118163). Joint Research Centre.

Seldon, A., Abidoye, O., & Metcalf, T. (2020). *The fourth education revolution reconsidered: Will artificial intelligence enrich or diminish humanity?.* Legend Press Ltd.

Selkrig, M., & Keamy, K. (2017). Creative pedagogy: A case for teachers' creative learning being at the centre. *Teaching Education, 28*(3), 317–332.

Selwyn, N. (2022). Digital degrowth: Toward radically sustainable education technology. *Learning, Media and Technology*, 1–14. https://doi.org/10.1080/17439884.2022.2159978

Zhai, X., Chu, X., Chai, C. S., Jong, M. S. Y., Istenic, A., Spector, M., Liu, J.-B., Yuan, J., & Li, Y. (2021). A review of Artificial Intelligence (AI) in education from 2010 to 2020. *Complexity, 2021*, e8812542. https://doi.org/10.1155/2021/8812542

Zhan, Z., Tong, Y., Lan, X., & Zhong, B. (2022). A systematic literature review of game-based learning in artificial intelligence education. *Interactive Learning Environments*, 1–22. https://doi.org/10.1080/10494820.2022.2115077

**Open Access** This chapter is licensed under the terms of the Creative Commons Attribution 4.0 International License (http://creativecommons.org/licenses/by/4.0/), which permits use, sharing, adaptation, distribution and reproduction in any medium or format, as long as you give appropriate credit to the original author(s) and the source, provide a link to the Creative Commons license and indicate if changes were made.

The images or other third party material in this chapter are included in the chapter's Creative Commons license, unless indicated otherwise in a credit line to the material. If material is not included in the chapter's Creative Commons license and your intended use is not permitted by statutory regulation or exceeds the permitted use, you will need to obtain permission directly from the copyright holder.

# 2

# Preserving Teacher and Student Agency: Insights from a Literature Review

## Alexandre Lepage and Simon Collin

**Abstract** This chapter is a comprehensive literature review that explores the influence of artificial intelligence (AI) on education and its implications for human agency. It begins by highlighting the potential advantages of incorporating AI in education, such as intelligent tutoring, learning assessment, and dropout prevention. The chapter then raises important questions regarding the roles of teachers and students in an AI-driven education system, contemplating whether AI can replace or enhance the capabilities of human educators. These inquiries initiate a discussion on the ethical considerations surrounding the deployment of AI in education.

---

A. Lepage (✉)
University of Montreal, Montreal, QC, Canada
e-mail: alexandre.lepage.2@umontreal.ca

S. Collin
University of Quebec in Montreal, Montreal, QC, Canada
e-mail: collin.simon@uqam.ca

To provide necessary context, the chapter offers definitions of AI in education and introduces two theoretical frameworks: the technician system theory and the concept of agency. The technician system theory suggests that as AI systems become more sophisticated, there is a risk of neglecting the complexity of teaching techniques and the expertise of human educators. The concept of agency is then presented as a means to comprehend and position human activity in relation to AI systems. The chapter explores agency from both the computer science and social science perspectives, emphasising the autonomy and decision-making abilities of both AI systems and individuals. With the focus on identifying AI applications that may limit teacher and student agency, the findings reveal that the integration of AI systems in education can lead to power imbalances and reduce the decision-making authority of teachers, shifting expertise to programmers and system designers. Likewise, student agency can be compromised by AI systems, particularly in task assignment and gamification.

Ultimately, this chapter underscores the significance of preserving human agency in the context of AI in education. It advocates for the design and implementation of AI-based tools that enhance agency rather than restrict it. The findings of the literature review shed light on the ethical implications and challenges associated with maintaining agency in the era of AI in education.

**Keywords** Agency · Teachers · Students · Literature review · Artificial intelligence algorithms

## Introduction

The process of automating tasks previously performed by people can present several potential hazards, many of which can be mitigated at the initial design phase. The emergence of artificial intelligence (AI) systems is expected to bring about significant changes in the roles and responsibilities of both instructors and students in the field of education. In the absence of precautions, certain AI-driven educational technologies have the potential to restrict instructors' autonomy in making pedagogical decisions, while also introducing errors in classification or judgement.

However, there are viable solutions available. This chapter provides an overview of the preliminary findings from a comprehensive examination of existing literature on the ethical concerns surrounding AI in education. The primary focus is on exploring the impact of AI on the autonomy and decision-making abilities of both teachers and students.

The field of education is susceptible to the swift advancement of AI methodologies and their capacity to execute progressively intricate tasks. The Beijing Consensus on AI in Education, as outlined by UNESCO (2019), recognises the potential advantages of AI in several tasks traditionally performed by students, instructors, and administrative personnel. AI can be applied in several ways in the field of education, such as smart tutoring, learning assessment, and student attrition prevention (Zawacki-Richter et al., 2019). These advancements prompt us to contemplate fresh inquiries: what if the educating faculty were freed from the laborious time dedicated to grading assignments? Is it possible for a student to receive immediate assistance, while at home, when they encounter a challenging maths problem? Can an AI support learners at the same level as a human teacher? These questions speak to some of the use cases for AI in education, but also highlight the ethical concerns that should be addressed when considering its implementation and widespread use.

This chapter aims to examine these concerns via the lens of preserving human agency (Engeström & Sannino, 2013), which is a significant challenge in the field of AI in education, on par with other challenges such as social justice, human complexity, and governance. We will sequentially provide contextual aspects, including definitions of AI in education, two theoretical benchmarks—the technician system and the idea of agency, and conclude with the findings of a literature review on the ethical concerns related to agency and AI in education.

## Artificial Intelligence Applied to Education

AI is a term that can mean many things. Applied to education, it aims to accomplish complex tasks such as providing feedback and the differentiation of learning experiences that, until recently, were only performed by human beings. AI can be considered a set of techniques with more or less defined contours. Its most common techniques fall under machine learning, which can be supervised, semi-supervised, or unsupervised (Taulli, 2019). Deep learning by artificial neural networks can be used to process so-called big data (i.e., data characterised by the speed at which it multiplies, its volume, and its diversity). Humble and Mozelius (2019) approach it by emphasising the interdisciplinary character that goes beyond computers, 'AIED is, as AI, an interdisciplinary field containing psychology, linguistics, neuroscience, education, anthropology and sociology with the goal of being a powerful tool for education and providing a deeper understanding of how learning occurs' (p. 1). AI can also be defined by qualities other than its computing methods, such as the functions it performs in a system. Loder and Nicholas (2018) present AI as 'computers which perform cognitive tasks usually associated with human minds, particularly learning and problem-solving' (p. 11). For Popenici and Kerr (2017), AI in education consists of 'computing systems that are able to engage in human-like processes such as learning, adapting, synthesising, self-correction and use of data for complex processing tasks' (p. 2). It is the latter definition that we will retain because it allows us to overcome the opposition between human intelligence and AI and to consider the complex interactions between the two.

## AI Through the Prism of the Technological System

We propose to consider these techniques from the angle of the technical system theory of Ellul (1977). According to this theory, techniques are constantly redefining the reality of the human experience. Ellul gives the example of television, made possible by the accumulation of techniques, whereby upon viewing, individuals end up no longer seeing these techniques. Television made possible a new form of communication that we ended up integrating, then trivialising to the point of not being interested in its operation any longer. In short, the techniques that made television possible, such as electricity or broadcasting antennas, end up taking root and redefining the actions and social relationships of its individual users. By applying a similar theory to AI, one might wonder if the complexity of AI techniques in education will change our relationship to the pedagogy and professional gestures specific to teaching. For instance, how might teachers reallocate their time if AI systems freed them from having to design and differentiate educational activities for their students? Furthermore, will educators stop being interested in docimology, the science of evaluation, because AI is capable of doing it for them? Unlike other educational technologies, the particularity of AI is that it is developed with the aim of accomplishing increasingly complex tasks, which then allows the teacher to concentrate on those tasks that AI does not handle well (e.g., high-complexity tasks that require a nuanced understanding of context, such as student relationships).

In this context, it is important to remember that teaching requires complex actions that are well-defined and familiar to educators. Hence, the integration of AI-based tools to accomplish these actions should not erode our understanding of this complexity, nor how we currently navigate and manage it in educational settings. As we embrace AI in education, we must be vigilant to not lose sight of the multifaceted nature of teaching by ensuring that technology complements, rather than overshadows, the contributions teachers bring to the educational landscape in terms of expertise and depth of knowledge.

## Agency to Understand and Situate Human Activity

The definition of AI in education by Popenici and Kerr (2017) introduces the idea that computer systems simulating human intelligence take place within human systems. We consider each of these systems as agents of one another. In computer science, the term agent designates a system with a certain amount of autonomy capable of carrying out actions that will have an impact on its environment. The future decision-making process is consequently impacted by these actions (Ferber, 1995, p. 13). This is one of the particularities of so-called intelligent complex systems:

they do not just reason (Ferber, 1995, p. 13); they act and transform their environment.

In the social sciences, the concept of agency also refers to a form of autonomy, but this time on the part of people. According to Engeström and Sannino (2013), agency is a voluntary search for transformation on the part of the subject and manifests itself in a polymotive problematic situation in which the subject evaluates and interprets the circumstances, makes decisions according to the interpretations, and executes those decisions (p. 7). For example, a teacher might have two seemingly conflicting goals; the desire to provide students with personalised feedback, while also wanting to return their grades as quickly as possible. In such situations, when motives or goals conflict, teachers can resolve them by taking actions that show their agency. For AI in education, this could mean empowering the student or teacher to have a greater impact through the use of AI systems. While this example describes an ideal scenario, current use cases for AI in education tend to focus on helping educators make better pedagogical decisions, automate time consuming or laborious tasks, or to analyse large data sets with the goal of improving learning outcomes.

## Research Question

At first glance, current educational use cases of AI are likely to encroach on the agency of students and teachers, especially when it comes to the selection and assessment of educational resources or activities. To address these initial challenges, we will attempt to answer the following research question: what use cases for AI in education are likely to limit the agency of teachers and students?

## Method: A Literature Review on Ethical Issues

This chapter is based on data collected during a systematic literature review project around the terms 'ethics, AI, and education' in the Google Scholar, Web of Science, Microsoft Academic, EBSCO Education, Dimensions databases, AI, and Scopus, and by completing with relevant references identified by the team (Michel & Le Nagard, 2019). Papers are peer-reviewed scientific articles or conference proceedings. They are written in French or English and published between 2010 and 2021 ($N = 58$). Articles were read and then segment coded using nVivo software by two people. While the review will be the subject of another publication, this chapter offers a specific, in-depth, and original analysis of the issues relating to the preservation of human agency. For the purposes of this chapter, there were 24 documents ($n = 24$) that were retained for analysis consisting of 62 coded segments.

## Results Related to the Agency of Teachers and Students

This section presents, in order, the results relating to teacher agency and then those relating to student agency. It aims to report, as faithfully and objectively as possible, without interpretation, the ideas conveyed in the literature.

### Results for Teacher Agency

Without specifying the type of AI tools in question, several of the documents consulted acknowledge the risk AI poses to reducing teacher agency as the development of complex computer systems shifts portions of their decision-making power to software development teams.

Integrating AI systems into education could exacerbate a power imbalance and create new inequalities. Similarly, AI systems can shift the centre of expertise from teachers and school administrators to programmers or system designers, the latter two being responsible for creating the models that diagnose learning outcomes, predict school achievement, and determine which recommendations will be displayed and to whom. (Berendt et al., 2020, p. 317). This is similar to the role of intelligent tutors who select teaching materials in place of the teacher and identify and diagnose at-risk students. Consider the example of a mathematics teacher who creates a series of exercises for solving quadratic equations. A priori, one would think that this is a task that could be automated or, at the very least, that existing teaching materials could be identified and reused. This may be true, but we should also try to understand why the teacher chose to create new material rather than reuse existing ones. One reason might be that the teacher is working with a multicultural group and cannot find materials with cultural references relevant to her class. The teacher might also choose to use a series of exercises that are too easy for her students for pedagogical considerations, such as providing students with a temporary boost to their confidence. As these examples demonstrate, teachers are able to exert their agency in polymotive situations whereas an AI-based system might only consider a didactic motive.

According to Berendt et al. (2020), the use of AI in education could also lead to a decline in teacher skills as they become too dependent on AI systems to the detriment of their own expertise. There is also reason to believe that automation bias (Parasuraman & Manzey, 2010), or the over reliance on automated decision-making systems, could become an issue for educators who lack the necessary training or agency to challenge the decisions of AI systems. Moreover, if this bias is not recognised by schools, they run the risk of encouraging the use of imperfect AI tools under the illusion that they are providing better predictions or results (Jones et al., 2020).

The agency always places the action in a broader context. Knox (2017) reminds us that software, algorithms, and databases are always used in broader contexts than it seems, but they are often seen as too detached from education as such. Student data is submitted, and teachers are encouraged to react to this data without having been part of the process responsible for producing it.

For Corrin et al. (2019), the use of AI-based tools must always involve human intervention for the review of contested decisions and classification errors. Gras (2019), drawing on the General Data Protection Regulation, speaks of the need for the maintenance of human control (p. 4), and Knox (2017) points out that the possibility of refusing data recommendations from an AI system must be preserved for teachers without the fear of negative consequences. Based on a similar concern, Sjödén (2020) goes so far as to question who should take precedence in the event of a discrepancy: such as an assessment grade, a recommended intervention, or a diagnosis of risk.

The importance of preserving agency is underlined by several of the consulted documents. Adams et al. (2021) talk about giving teachers the choice of whether or not to use AI-based tools. Aiken and Epstein (2000) state: 'at all cost we must preserve the human capacity to solve problems and think rationally' (p. 166). Holmes et al. (2021) invite us not to fall into a glorification of progress in computer systems that would diminish the role of humans. Yet, Smuha (2020) contrasts with the other reviewed documents by stating that as long as educators retain the ability to choose whether or not to use and trust AI recommendations, then agency can be increased: 'As long as human beings can meaningfully decide when and under what conditions decisions are delegated to an AI-system, human agency is not only preserved, but can even be empowered' (Smuha, 2020, p. 8). Finally, amongst all the consulted documents, there is consensus on the need for AI developers to design tools that increase user agency, not restrict it.

## Student Agency Results

Students should also be able to choose whether or not to act in accordance with the recommendations of an AI system (Roberts et al., 2017). This is because, within the learning environment, the use of AI can reduce student agency. According to Bulger (2016), this is the case when an AI system assigns school tasks. In higher education settings, Roberts et al. (2017) highlight the risk of infantilising students if AI systems gamify learning experiences when it is neither necessary nor wanted by learners. West et al. (2020) also mention this risk, emphasising the relevance of student voices in the process of regulating learning. Their perceptions, comments, and experiences should be considered when making pedagogical decisions and should not be diminished by the use of AI systems. Similarly, students should also have the choice of whether or not to accept AI recommendations.

Currently, predictive systems that rely on data can lead to erroneous programme or course recommendations for students (Jones et al., 2020). This is generally a problem of filter bubbles, where recommendation algorithms succeed in identifying preferences from previous data sets, but fail to suggest new interests. This is the case for recommendations on music platforms or streaming services where these types of algorithms actually limit agency (Jones et al., 2020) or, at the very least, participate in redefining the environment in which agency is exercised. Regan and Jesse (2019) point out that these uses, even if they may seem trivial, have an impact on people's ability to manage their lives freely.

Regan and Jesse (2019), building on the work of Kerr and Earle (2013), present three types of predictions that can affect agency: predictions that allow people to anticipate negative consequences, predictions that direct people towards specific decisions, and prescriptive predictions that reduce the possible choices people can make. According to Regan and Jesse (2019), consequence-based predictions reduce people's agency a little, while prescriptive predictions reduce it a lot. Take, for example, the difference between a system that automatically recommends a series of learning resources without hiding other potential resources and another that selects and integrates them into a so-called personalised learning pathway. The first maintains a certain agency, while the second reduces it on the basis of making decisions on behalf of the learner.

At the level of didactic use, Sjödén (2020) notes that AI-based systems can integrate false information into the learning environment. He presents three types of processes that AI systems could use and which could pose ethical problems: cases where the systems lie, i.e., present deliberately inaccurate information; cases where they hide information by selecting which data to present; and cases where they maintain erroneous beliefs. Sjödén (2020) asks the question, 'To what extent are such illusions ethically justifiable to maintain?' (p. 293). Here, the link with agency stems from the authenticity of the environment in which agency is exercised. This raises the question, is agency supported by partial or false information really agency?

Reiss (2021), drawing on Puddifoot and O'Donnell (2018), points out that tools that pursue an intention to facilitate learning can hinder the intellectual activity necessary for the formation of concepts:

> Puddifoot and O'Donnell (2018) argue that too great a reliance on technologies to store information for us – information that in previous times we would have had to remember – may be counterproductive, resulting in missed opportunities for the memory systems of students to form abstractions and generate insights from newly learned information. (p. 4)

Even in the presence of tools aimed at facilitating the task of learners, it may be temporarily relevant to maintain a specific intellectual activity for the development of certain logical structures of thought. For example, a tool that pre-identifies the important passages in a text to avoid the student having to read it completely might not be desirable if the pedagogical intention is to develop the student's ability to synthesise. Similar to the concerns raised before the introduction of the calculator, Smuha (2020) talks about the risk of developing intellectual laziness by interacting with more efficient machines for the performance of certain tasks. According to parents of students, some tools could even be obstacles to learning if students do not develop a critical perspective or place too much trust in them (Qin et al., 2020)

> However, some parents worry that AIED systems may make students overly dependent on AI-based systems and lack independent thinking, which brings out parents' unwillingness to continuously trust in AIED systems. (p. 1699)

Certain risks are added when it comes to higher education. Overly guided systems that interfere in the organisation of school work could be perceived as infantilising by stakeholders (Roberts et al., 2017). This risk is also supported by West et al. (2020), who assert that learners must be perceived as people capable of regulating their own learning. Roberts et al. (2017) seek to ensure that students are never forced to act in accordance with the recommendations of a system or on the basis of its performance indicators. It is also important to emphasise that any systems used be valid, reliable, and capable of performing the tasks for which they were designed in a real context (Smuha, 2020).

## Discussion: Some Nuances and Ways to Guard Against Risks

In light of the results, this section systematically returns to two of the elements addressed earlier, namely the technical system and the concept of agency. It also presents some ways to support the development of AI in education while preserving the agency of students and teachers.

### Discussion of the Technical System

The emergence of AI, primarily driven by machine learning techniques, enables tools that increasingly shape the context in which individuals engage. As these tools advance, they progressively define and influence the educational landscape. In line with Ellul's perspective (1977), teaching can be viewed as a set of techniques and strategies encompassing pedagogical approaches, evaluation methods, but also digital tools. However, as these digital tools, particularly those involving AI, grow in complexity, there's a tendency for the underlying intricacies to become obscured, opaque, or even dismissed entirely. In this sense, AI-based computer systems applying these techniques in an educational context cannot be considered only as tools. They redefine several parameters of the educational situation, including the time required to accomplish a task, the need to memorise certain information, the need to ask for help in order to accomplish a task, or the possibilities of social interactions.

The use of AI in education also challenges the powers of educational stakeholders. Some tools represent 'a form of privatization and commercialism by shifting control over curriculum and pedagogy from teachers and schools to for-profit corporations' (Saltman, 2020, p. 199).

While this shift of power may be desirable for reasons of efficiency or innovation, it must be done cautiously by assessing all the potential consequences that may result from such actions. Likewise, the idea that AI can only be seen as a way of improving the teaching and learning experience should be challenged. Not only is this conception insufficient to describe the impact these tools could have on teaching and learning, but it fails to consider AI as a set of techniques that alter the actions of students and teachers, while also failing to acknowledge that teaching and learning are themselves products of techniques.

### Discussion in Relation to Agency

Agency, as we have presented it, involves taking action in situations with conflicting motives. Any use of AI that removes options to take such initiatives limits agency. However, it is possible to mitigate this risk by having AI developers consider the importance of student and teacher agency at the earliest stages of their tool development. According to Kerr and Earle (2013), this could be done by designing systems that empower users to exercise their own judgement and choice rather than relying on predictive systems of consequence, preference, or preemption. This is why, within the realm of learning analytics, the development of dashboards must incorporate the real needs of learners.

## Avenues for the Development of AI-Based Tools that Preserve Agency

The results of our literature review raise several risks relating to the maintenance of human agency through the use of AI in education, both for teachers and for students. To counter these risks, we propose three recommendations for designing AI-based educational technologies that preserve, or even reinforce, human agency.

First, AI should not be responsible for making autonomous educational decisions, but rather, focused on improving the quality of information that people use in order to make more informed decisions. This can be done by presenting the probable consequences of decisions (Regan & Jesse, 2019), and providing transparency on the data utilised to make those decisions.

Second, with respect to the assessment of learning, the use of AI for rapid, personalised, and frequent feedback, in contexts where teacher feedback is unlikely, seems promising. As in other AI use cases, these systems must be transparent, in particular to students, regarding how the feedback was produced. Consistent with the first recommendation, assessment systems should be focused on providing students with quality feedback and not making decisions related to grading or being used to replace professional judgement.

Finally, in regard to learning aids intended for students, they can be developed with the caveat that this usage of AI seems uncertain at the moment. The pedagogical intentions of the curricula do not always allow, at a fine-grained level, to distinguish which intellectual activity is essential from the instrumental or already acquired. The uses of AI aimed at engaging students in techno-creative projects (Romero et al., 2017) and participating in their own skill development seem more promising in the short term, particularly when combined with uses previously intended for the teacher. In higher education, there is the added risk of infantilising or providing an excess of guidance, which highlights the need for robust learning analytics to determine the real needs of students.

## Conclusion

In an educational situation, both teachers and students demonstrate agency on a daily basis. Despite numerous efforts to model educational problems and automate solutions (e.g., the evaluation of learning), it must be kept in mind that these problems can be approached from several points of view that often involve intangible human dimensions and conflicting motives. It is through agency that these situations are resolved on a daily basis. We must therefore avoid the reductionist trap of designing didactic tools detached from the context in which they are used.

While there are a number of recommendations for doing this, we have proposed three: (1) use AI to improve the quality of information rather than making educational decisions, (2) use AI for formative feedback and not for certification assessment, particularly when training students and teachers from a critical perspective, and (3) favouring uses that engage students and allow them to develop a critical perspective on the role of AI in education.

# References

Adams, C., Pente, P., Lemermeyer, G., & Rockwell, G. (2021). Artificial intelligence ethics guidelines for K-12 education: A review of the global landscape. In I. Roll, D. McNamara, S. Sosnovsky, R. Luckin & V. Dimitrova (Éds.), *International conference on artificial intelligence in education* (Vol. 12749, pp. 24–28). Springer.

Aiken, R. M., & Epstein, R. G. (2000). Ethical guidelines for AI in education: Starting a conversation. *International Journal of Artificial Intelligence in Education, 11*, 163–176.

Berendt, B., Littlejohn, A., & Blakemore, M. (2020). AI in education: Learner choice and fundamental rights. *Learning, Media and Technology, 45*(3), 312–324.

Bulger, M. (2016). Personalized learning: The conversations we're not having. *Data & Society, 22*(1), 1–29.

Corrin, L., Kennedy, G., French, S., Shum, S. B., Kitto, K., Pardo, A., West, D., Mirriahi, N., & Colvin, C. (2019). *The ethics of learning analytics in Australian higher education.* University of Melbourne CSHE.

Ellul, J. (1977). *Le système technicien.* Calmann-Levy.

Engeström, Y., & Sannino, A. (2013). La volition et l'agentivité transformatrice : perspective théorique de l'activité. *Revue internationale du CRIRES : innover dans la tradition de Vygotsky, 1*(1), 4–19.

Ferber, J. (1995). Les systèmes multi-agents intelligents : Vers une intelligence collective. Inter-Editions.

Gras, B. (2019). Éthique des Learning Analytics. *Distances et médiations des savoirs, 26*, 1–8. https://doi.org/10.4000/dms.3768

Holmes, W., Porayska-Pomsta, K., Holstein, K., Sutherland, E., Baker, T., Shum, S. B., Santos, O. C., Rodrigo, M. T., Cukurova, M., Bittencourt,

I. I., & Koedinger, K. R. (2021). Ethics of AI in education: Towards a community-wide framework. *International Journal of Artificial Intelligence in Education, 32*(2), 504–526.

Humble, N., & Mozelius, P. (2019). Teacher-supported AI or AI-supported teachers? In *Proceedings of the European conference on the impact of artificial intelligence and robotics* (pp. 157–164). Academic Conferences and Publishing International Limited.

Jones, K. M. L., Rubel, A., & LeClere, E. (2020). A matter of trust: Higher education institutions as information fiduciaries in an age of educational data mining and learning analytics. *Journal of the Association for Information Science and Technology, 71*(10), 1227–1241.

Kerr, I., & Earle, J. (2013). Prediction, preemption, presumption: How big data threatens big picture privacy. *Stanford Law Review Online, 66*, 65–72.

Knox, J. (2017). Data power in education: Exploring critical awareness with the "Learning Analytics Report Card." *Television & New Media, 18*(8), 734–752.

Loder, J., & Nicholas, L. (2018). *Confronting Dr Robot—Creating a people-powered future for AI in health* (p. 38). Nesta Health Lab.

Michel, G., & Le Nagard, E. (2019). Favoriser la sérendipité pour des recherches plus créatives. *Décisions Marketing, 1*, 5–9.

Parasuraman, R., & Manzey, D. H. (2010). Complacency and bias in human use of an attentional integration. *Human Factors, 52*(3), 381–410.

Popenici, S. A. D., & Kerr, S. (2017). Exploring the impact of artificial intelligence on teaching and learning in higher education. *Research and Practice in Technology Enhanced Learning, 12*(22), 1–13.

Puddifoot, K., & O'Donnell, C. (2018). Human memory and the limits of technology in education. *Educational Theory, 68*(6), 643–655.

Qin, F., Li, K., & Yan, J. (2020). Understanding user trust in artificial intelligence-based educational systems: Evidence from China. *British Journal of Educational Technology, 51*(5), 1693–1710.

Regan, P. M., & Jesse, J. (2019). Ethical challenges of edtech, big data and personalized learning: Twenty-first century student sorting and tracking. *Ethics and Information Technology, 21*(3), 167–179.

Reiss, M. J. (2021). The use of AI in education: Practicalities and ethical considerations. *London Review of Education, 19*(1), 1–14.

Roberts, L. D., Chang, V., & Gibson, D. (2017). Ethical considerations in adopting a university-and system-wide approach to data and learning analytics. In B. Kei Daniel (Éd.), *Big data and learning analytics in higher education* (pp. 89–108). Springer.

Romero, M., Lille, B., & Patiño, A. (2017). *Usages créatifs du numérique pour l'apprentissage au XXIe siècle*. Presses de l'Université du Québec.

Saltman, K. J. (2020). Artificial intelligence and the technological turn of public education privatization: In defence of democratic education. *London Review of Education, 18*(2), 196–208.

Sjödén, B. (2020). When lying, hiding and deceiving promotes learning—A case for augmented intelligence with augmented ethics. In I. I. Bittencourt, M. Cukurova, K. Muldner, R. Luckin, & E. Millán (Éds.), *Artificial Intelligence in education* (Vol. 12164, p. 291–295). Springer.

Smuha, N. A. (2020). Trustworthy artificial intelligence in education: Pitfalls and pathways. *SSRN Electronic Journal*. https://doi.org/10.2139/ssrn.3742421

Taulli, T. (2019). *Artificial Intelligence basics: A non-technical introduction*. Hurry.

UNESCO. (2019). *Beijing consensus on artificial intelligence and education*. https://en.unesco.org/themes/ict-education

West, D., Luzeckyj, A., Toohey, D., Vanderlelie, J., & Searle, B. (2020). Do academics and university administrators really know better? The ethics of positioning student perspectives in learning analytics. *Australasian Journal of Educational Technology, 36*(2), 60–70.

Zawacki-Richter, O., Marín, V. I., Bond, M., & Gouverneur, F. (2019). Systematic review of research on artificial intelligence applications in higher education–where are the educators? *International Journal of Educational Technology in Higher Education, 16*(1), 39.

**Open Access** This chapter is licensed under the terms of the Creative Commons Attribution 4.0 International License (http://creativecommons.org/licenses/by/4.0/), which permits use, sharing, adaptation, distribution and reproduction in any medium or format, as long as you give appropriate credit to the original author(s) and the source, provide a link to the Creative Commons license and indicate if changes were made.

The images or other third party material in this chapter are included in the chapter's Creative Commons license, unless indicated otherwise in a credit line to the material. If material is not included in the chapter's Creative Commons license and your intended use is not permitted by statutory regulation or exceeds the permitted use, you will need to obtain permission directly from the copyright holder.

# 3

# Learning Artificial Intelligence Through Open Educational Resources

Frédéric Alexandre, Marie-Helene Comte, Aurélie Lagarrigue, and Thierry Viéville

**Abstract** This chapter discusses the creation and impact of a Massive Open Online Course (MOOC) titled 'Artificial Intelligence with Intelligence (IAI)' aimed at fostering a culture of AI understanding and participation in ethical debates. The chapter first addresses the rationale behind developing the MOOC and the importance of citizen training in AI, particularly concerning ethical considerations surrounding algorithmic decision-making. This chapter also emphasises the need to reevaluate human intelligence in the broader context of AI advancements and probes the transformative nature of AI across various domains of

---

F. Alexandre (✉) · M.-H. Comte · A. Lagarrigue · T. Viéville
Mnemosyne team, Inria U. Bordeaux, IMN and CNRS, Talence, France
e-mail: Frederic.Alexandre@inria.fr

M.-H. Comte
e-mail: marie-helene.comte@inria.fr

A. Lagarrigue
e-mail: aurelie.lagarrigue@inria.fr

T. Viéville
e-mail: Thierry.Vieville@inria.fr

life. Three perspectives are considered concerning the integration of AI in education: adapting the learning experience, using AI as a scientific tool for studying human learning, and critically examining its problems. Citizen education is crucial to understanding the scientific and technical elements of AI, especially in the context of algorithmic decision-making ethics. The chapter's focus on AI and citizen education is key. It emphasises the need for critical thinking to understand how AI technologies affect daily life. The chapter advocates AI training to help people understand how AI works and generate informed opinions about its potential and limitations.

**Keywords** AI literacy · Citizen education · MOOC · Online learning · Ethics

## Introduction

AI in education can be approached from three parallel perspectives. First, it can be used to adapt the learning experience by designing tools that take into account different learner characteristics or the digital learning analytics resulting from their interaction with systems. Such systems could have the potential to support some teachers' tasks and allow them to intervene in more complex aspects of student learning. Secondly, AI can be used as a scientific tool to better understand human learning phenomena, by modelling the learner. Finally, AI can be considered from a critical perspective. This chapter presents these three complimentary, but not mutually exclusive, perspectives to better understand the challenges of AI in an educational setting.

The latest research combining education and digital sciences makes it possible to understand the potential and limitations of artificial intelligence (AI) in the education domain. This research highlights the potential for designing AI systems that can enhance their learning capabilities and foster critical thinking (Roux et al., 2020; Viéville, 2019). Furthermore, it underscores AI's capacity, as an instructive entity, to understand the intricacies of human learning as well as its ability to build more proficient users of these ubiquitous tools (Viéville & Guitton, 2020).

## AI as an Adaptive Learning Tool

Learning can be made adaptive through the use of algorithms that analyse student learning analytics, such as quiz results or software usage data, to adapt to individual learners by modifying difficulty levels or curating content. Other adaptive systems can be made using external cameras or brain–computer interfaces, which allow algorithms to further analyse behaviour through sensors. This principle of adaptation is at the heart of digital pedagogy and is often integrated alongside gamification strategies where the learner participates in an educational game either solo or in collaboration with other learners (Giraudon et al., 2020).

The KidLearn Project offers a variety of learning activities whose multiple variants involve the addition or subtraction of whole or decimal numbers designed and implemented by mathematical didacticians. These variants are organised in the form of a graph of increasing difficulty, respecting Vygotsky's concept of the proximal zone of development (Vygotsky, 1978). This concept posits that optimal learning, as evidenced by a student's performance over time, occurs in a zone that is neither too challenging, which can lead to discouragement, nor too easy, which can result in boredom. In a similar fashion, this concept can be applied utilising algorithms that automatically adapt to the learner. These elements can be integrated into the algorithm, which will automatically adapt to the learner's progression (Oudeyer et al., 2020).

While the development of these applications remains limited, the ongoing scientific research provides a crucial stage for initial reflection, aiding in understanding the processes of knowledge acquisition and appropriation. Indeed, to implement this adaptive approach systematically, it is essential to formalise both the knowledge and know-how, or practices, to be taught. This necessitates the explanation and structuring of task types and problem-solving techniques. Moreover, it is necessary to ensure that the learning process is not burdened with extraneous cognitive tasks unrelated to the activity itself. Adaptive learning should also occur within a context bound by equipment availability, personnel training, and screen usage limitations.

The positive effects of machine learning are numerous. Primarily, we notice that adaptive learning positively enhances learner engagement, as diverse interactions with the content provide additional opportunities for comprehensive understanding. Indeed, the fact that the difficulty level of a learning experience can be adapted to an individual learner makes it possible to limit or even avoid discouragement or weariness. Also, unlike a human, the machine does not 'judge', which can help maintain the learners' engagement. However, this type of learning may require a substantial effort on the teacher's behalf if the design does not take into account the student's cognitive load. There is also the risk that students may lose sight of the intended learning goals if the gamification aspects are too prominent.

Adaptive tools incorporating AI principles should allow teachers to devote more time to students who need it most, while the rest of the class engages in self-directed learning activities. These tools also allow teachers to shift away from traditional knowledge transmission methods, such as self-assessed multimedia content and automated training exercises, and focus more on other pedagogical approaches such as project-based learning. Compared to non-adaptive digital tools, i.e. those without machine learning, the degree of autonomous learning can be significantly higher and more widely applicable, incorporating comprehensive skills development paths. These tools also meet a need in the context of distance learning situations and prompt a reevaluation of how school work time is currently organised.

However, it is also crucial to highlight the potential misuse of this data: the pervasive tracking and categorisation of learners, the temptation to reduce the number of school staff, and the exacerbation of inequalities related to illiteracy (Allemang et al., 2020). Attention should also be paid to how these digital learning practices might blend or merge with other online behaviours, such as shopping, streaming videos, or reading, thereby influencing or altering their original purposes.

## AI as a Model for Understanding Human Learning

The ability to collect and interpret learning analytics could lead to improved learning, whether these metrics are used by the learner or by the teacher for self or external regulation (Romero, 2019). The use of learning analytics could also make it possible to better understand human learning methods in the long term. These learning insights can be detected using software by measuring mouse movements or finger clicks, keyboard input, or by sensors used in teaching situations with or without a computer (e.g. camera, microphone, accelerometer, or GPS). Exploiting these measures requires not only the formalisation of the learning task itself but also the modelling of both the task and the learner, not holistically, but within the framework of a specific task.

The use of learning analytics in digital learning environments makes it possible to model the learning task, but also the learner's activity within the task. Machine learning algorithms rely on fairly sophisticated models. These mechanisms are not necessarily confined to supervised learning, where answers are adjusted from examples provided with the solution, but also work by 'reinforcement' where the system infers causes that explain the positive (called rewards[1]) or negative feedback during learning by building an internal model of the task to be performed. These models are operational in that they make it possible to create effective algorithms that adjust their parameters. One might wonder if such models can effectively represent aspects of human learning. In neuroscience, these computational models already represent our brain's functional processes as calculations or information processing mechanisms at the neuronal level, thereby augmenting our comprehension of such cognitive functions.

This area of using computer science and AI as formalisation tools to model human learning, called 'computational education science' (Romero et al., 2020), is still in its infancy, but has already revealed its

---

[1] In the context of reinforcement learning, the concept of 'rewards' encompasses both positive and negative outcomes. This extends beyond the traditional understanding of reinforcement in psychology, which typically associates reinforcement with positive outcomes only.

potential for the learning sciences. This is why research is carried out in a transdisciplinary manner utilising both digital sciences and cognitive neurosciences to explore these potentialities.

## AI and Citizen Education

In order to 'master' the digital technologies in the sense of Giraudon et al. (2020) and understand their application (Atlan et al., 2019; Romero, 2018), it is important to be initiated into the scientific and technical functioning of hardware and software computing objects. In a similar fashion, the integration of AI technologies into our daily lives calls for the development of critical thinking in young people (Viéville & Guitton, 2020).

It is important to understand that in AI, the outcome of data processing by the algorithms is not solely tied to their programming. The desired functions are not implemented only using instructions, but also by providing data from which the parameters are adjusted to obtain the desired calculation. Depending on the degree of program autonomy, there may even be unintended consequences as has been the case in chatbot systems that have learned, through poor quality corpora, to produce unethical comments on social media. Legally, it is also important to be familiar with the implications of interacting with a 'cobot' or a robotic mechanism in our daily lives. Consider, for example, a medical machine whose function would be to help inform therapeutic decision-making in response to different degrees of urgency. This situation, and others like it, stress just how much the chain of responsibility between design, construction, installation, configuration, and use is infinitely more complex than the behaviour of a non-autonomous machine.

AI training should help develop the knowledge and skills necessary to comprehend how AI works and enable individuals to develop informed opinions on the capabilities and limitations of its use. It is in the face of these challenges that the MOOC Artificial Intelligence with Intelligence was created as a way to familiarise educators with computer science in a non-technical manner and illustrate how AI can contribute to developing skills (Alexandre et al., 2021). Educational tools exist and continue

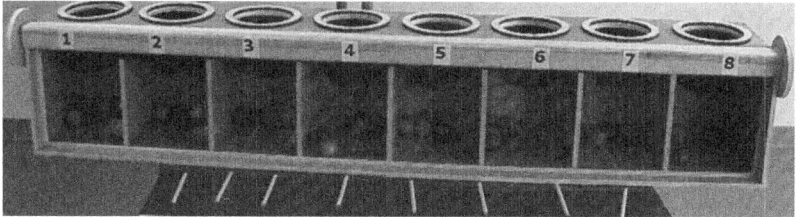

**Fig. 3.1** An example of an unplugged activity for experimenting with a reinforcement learning algorithm

to be developed that gradually introduce learners to the operation of AI. Figure 3.1 shows a minimalist 'machine', developed by Pixees and built by Snzzur.fr, that utilises blue and red balls to simulate the use of algorithms in an 'unplugged' game. The game's construction plans are freely available and can be inexpensively reproduced using basic tools. It has been established that learning computer science principles in an 'unplugged' way, i.e. removing oneself from machine interactions to actively focus on the underlying concepts, makes it easier to understand the working mechanisms of AI.

## A Shift in Our Way of Thinking

Since the beginning of computing, we have seen our way of learning and teaching evolve. For example, is it still necessary to learn calculation when calculators are readily available? While it may be essential for understanding arithmetic operations, the need to become proficient calculators is lessened in the face of ubiquitous technologies. On the other hand, we will always need to calculate orders of magnitude to ensure that the calculation is relevant and that we have not made any errors when posting or obtaining the result.

These changes in human activity are found as we automate processes that are a matter of human intelligence. When we are content to use AI algorithms without seeking to understand their main operating principles and their implications for our lives, we risk losing individual and collective intelligence. We will become reliant on their mechanisms, thinking less for ourselves, and developing less of the critical spirit essential to the formation of autonomous and enlightened citizens. This is the whole point of understanding how AI works (Roux et al., 2020). If, instead, we seek to understand and master these processes, then the possibility of delegating what, in human intelligence, is mechanisable can offer us the chance to consciously free ourselves from automaticities in order to devote our intelligence to higher-level goals and more humanly important issues.

# References

Alexandre, F., Becker, J., Comte, M. H., Lagarrigue, A., Liblau, R., Romero, M., & Viéville, T. (2021). Why, what and how to help each citizen to understand artificial intelligence? *KI-Künstliche Intelligenz, 35*(2), 191–199.

Allemang, D., Gandon, F., & Hendler, J. (2020). *Semantic web for the working ontologist: Effective modeling for linked data, RDFS, and OWL* (3rd ed.). Association for Computing Machinery. https://hal.inria.fr/hal-02939606, https://doi.org/10.1145/3382097. ISBN 978-1-4503-7617-4.

Atlan, C., Archambault, J. P., Banus, O., Bardeau, F., Blandeau, A., Cois, A., Courbin, M., Giraudon, G., Lefèvre, S.-C., Létard, V., Masse, B., Masseglia, F., Ninassi, B., de Quatrebarbes, S., Romero, M., Roy, D., & Viéville, T. (2019). *Apprentissage de la pensée informatique: de la formation des enseignant·e·s à la formation de tou·te·s les citoyen·ne·s*. Revue de l'EPI.

Giraudon, G., Guitton, P., Romero, M., Roy, D., & Viéville, T. (2020). *Éducation et numérique, Défis et enjeux*. Inria.

Oudeyer, P. Y., Clément, B., Roy, D., & Sauzéon, H. (2020). Projet KidLearn: Vers une personnalisation motivante des parcours d'apprentissage. *Bulletin de l'Association Française pour l'Intelligence Artificielle*, 51–55.

Romero, M. (2018). Développer la pensée informatique pour démystifier l'intelligence artificielle. *1024, Bulletin de la société informatique de France, 12*, 67–75.

Romero, M. (2019). Analyser les apprentissages à partir des traces. *Distances et médiations des savoirs* (26).

Romero, M., Alexandre, F., Viéville, T., & Giraudon, G. (2020). LINE - Mnémosyne: Des neurosciences computationnelles aux sciences de l'éducation computationnelles pour la modélisation du cerveau de l'apprenant et du contexte de l'activité d'apprentissage. *Bulletin de l'Association Française pour l'Intelligence Artificielle*, AFIA.

Roux, L., Romero, M., Alexandre, F., & Viéville, T. (2020). Les hauts de Otesia. *Binaire*.

Viéville, T. (2019). Mais comment éduquer les garçons à l'équité des genres au niveau informatique et numérique. Éducation à la mixité: Et les garçons? Un rêve pour les filles et les garçons. *La Science*.

Viéville, T., & Guitton, P. (2020). Quels sont les liens entre IA et Éducation? *Binaire*.

Vygotsky, L. S. (1978). *Mind in society: The development of higher psychological processes*. Harvard University Press.

**Open Access** This chapter is licensed under the terms of the Creative Commons Attribution 4.0 International License (http://creativecommons.org/licenses/by/4.0/), which permits use, sharing, adaptation, distribution and reproduction in any medium or format, as long as you give appropriate credit to the original author(s) and the source, provide a link to the Creative Commons license and indicate if changes were made.

The images or other third party material in this chapter are included in the chapter's Creative Commons license, unless indicated otherwise in a credit line to the material. If material is not included in the chapter's Creative Commons license and your intended use is not permitted by statutory regulation or exceeds the permitted use, you will need to obtain permission directly from the copyright holder.

# 4

# Digital Acculturation in the Era of Artificial Intelligence

### Michel Durampart, Philippe Bonfils, and Margarida Romero

**Abstract** This chapter examines AI integration in education, concentrating on acculturation, as a broad movement of appropriating digital tools. The chapter emphasises principals' involvement in supporting AI potential in schools and the complex interplay between digital technology and education. The chapter describes teachers' transition from personal to educational digital use across three phases of digital acculturation. It emphasises professional development by highlighting problems and motivations. The last part of the chapter discusses digital acculturation in AI and education, including medical expertise, vocational training, and special education. It finishes by analysing educational

---

M. Durampart (✉) · P. Bonfils
Université de Toulon, Toulon, France
e-mail: michel.durampart@univ-tln.fr

P. Bonfils
e-mail: philippe.bonfils@univ-tln.fr

M. Romero
Université Côte d'Azur, Nice, France
e-mail: margarida.romero@univ-cotedazur.fr; margarida.romero@unice.fr

© The Author(s) 2024
A. Urmeneta and M. Romero (eds.), *Creative Applications of Artificial Intelligence in Education*, Palgrave Studies in Creativity and Culture,
https://doi.org/10.1007/978-3-031-55272-4_4

platform organisational changes and AI's ability to change learning dynamics and interfaces, raising new considerations about global education systems.

**Keywords** Acculturation · Digital culture · Educational technologies · Digital competencies

## Introduction

The uses of educational technologies, of which artificial intelligence (AI) is a part, require a pedagogical reflection on the planning and orchestration of the learning activities. The representations and the culture of the actors, teachers, and students can impact the school organisation and are points to be taken into account in the integration of AI in educational settings (Bellas et al., 2023). This chapter pursues two objectives: on the one hand, to define acculturation to AI as a vast movement of appropriation of digital tools; and, on the other hand, in the light of the work of the Mediterranean Institute of Information and Communication (IMSIC), to analyse the digital acculturation in the AI era.

Acculturation is defined in broad terms as "the processes by which different cultural groups adapt to one another" (Brown & Zagefka, 2011, p. 131), but also the process of adoption of cultural artefacts such as digital technologies and the reduction of the digital divide of certain cultural groups (Vassilakopoulou & Hustad, 2023). The process of acculturation in the context of artificial intelligence concerns not only edtech professionals but the different educational stakeholders who, having developed their careers absent of AI, are now adapting to new educational practices and different types of teaching and learning processes.

## Digital Acculturation from the Lens of Information and Communication Studies

Information and communication sciences have helped to highlight that the relationship between digital technology and education is complex, iterative, and cross sectional (Bonfils, 2020; Durampart, 2016; Giraudon et al., 2020). In this context, researchers from the IMSIC research lab found that digital artefacts intended for learning activities (Bernard et al., 2018) tend to cause tensions within the school organisation. School organisation is highly structured in secondary education, which creates a tension when innovative approaches are required to adapt to the opportunities afforded by AI. In this context, Meyer et al. (2023) consider the importance of the principal's role in ensuring that the school's pedagogical team is able to create the necessary conditions for change.

Over the course of twelve years of research at the IMSIC laboratory, we found the concept of digital acculturation to be useful in classifying the broad movement of appropriation of digital technologies influencing pedagogy and educational practices. This concept arose as a useful heuristic in order to characterise an unstable, discontinuous, and diverse movement that encompasses the adoption of digital technology across a wide range of activities and approaches within the educational context. In this way, scholars working on such topics recommend thinking about "digital acculturation" rather than "digital culture" (Durampart, 2016). The primary challenge lies in integrating this ostensibly digital culture within the framework of economic and social well-being, where digital inclusion encompasses the broader capacity of individuals to effectively mobilise these technologies—a critical skill as the knowledge economy continues to expand its influence (Durampart, 2016). While it is difficult to recreate the breadth of the disciplines and initiatives in which we have been involved, we can retrace a few significant steps and milestones that have helped us better comprehend the concept of digital acculturation.

The studies of Pélissier et al. (2018) shows that only a minority of students exploit their "digital culture" with a view to integration and professional orientation, while showing the potential to consider creative pedagogies for improving the learners' experience. Even if formal learning is crucial to reduce the variance in proficiency levels among social actors, it remains necessary for them to develop new creative practices in the use of AI in contexts other than those related to leisure and interpersonal relationships. The challenge of digital acculturation would therefore refer to a form of unstable, heterogeneous and disseminated economic, social, and cultural capital. It is constantly called into play and questioned, with different modes of adoption, in various contexts, while also referring to successive or alternating forms of formal and informal stacked learning.

## The Three Levels of Digital Acculturation

The impetus for IMSIC's research projects on digital acculturation derived from a study carried out as part of the Provence-Alpes-Côte d'Azur (PACA) region's ICT observatory (Pélissier et al., 2013). Further insights were gathered from the Numécole project, an initiative from the Ministry of National Education to identify the digital uses of technology among French teachers with the aim of improving student outcomes and facilitating teachers' pedagogical practices (Durampart, 2016) It is from these projects that we developed the following framework to better understand the role of digital acculturation and its role in effectively navigating and utilising digital tools. This framework comprises three distinct levels; the acquisition of technological knowledge, the interaction between personal and professional uses of technology, and the use of technology in pedagogical practices.

### First Level of Digital Acculturation

At the initial level of digital acculturation, teachers utilise digital tools for personal use rather than for interchange or sharing. The first stage of digital acculturation is concerned with knowledge acquisition through training. 82% of instructors between the ages of 31 and 50 (representing 77% of our respondents) completed pre-service teacher training.[1] 73% of them claim they use technology frequently, but 68% complain about insufficient training overall. Again, these teachers are more likely to

---

[1] The data derives from a Numécole research program occuring between 2014 and 2016. A questionnaire was sent to teachers in November 2015 with the aim of providing a quantitative analysis of experimentation with digital applications in the PACA region. Over 200 teachers responded representing 80 classes.

utilise information and communication technology (ICT) as a personal tool than as a tool for trade or sharing. Examples include software trials, do-it-yourself projects, self-learning, as well as shared learning in co-learning and multi-learning circumstances. These encounters, characterised by a variety of demands and expectations aimed at simplifying everyday life, serve as barriers to implementing these talents professionally. As a result, the absence of professional training makes developing an advanced degree of expertise impossible.

## Second Level of Digital Acculturation

The integration of digital technology at the second level of digital acculturation seeks to promote the interaction between school and home and puts a range of technological applications at the service of educational activities. This level is situated in an unsuccessful relationship between private, personal, and domestic learning and those of the professional or educational world. The so-called innovative digital initiatives (Project Incubateurs, 2018–2019) are part of a worldwide ambition to employ digital media to enhance continuity between school and home.

However, moving digital applications from the private to the professional realm requires rehabilitation and instructional supervision. As one teacher commented on her survey, "The tablets are entering the establishment (i.e. schools) because they have entered our lives" (Durampart, 2016). This teacher also highlighted the importance of combining tablet use with an effective method of information retrieval to maximise the devices' potential in the classroom. This phenomenon, known as porosity, refers to the permeation of digital technology into the school environment, directly impacting the organisation of schools.

## Third Level of Digital Acculturation

The third level of digital acculturation involves teaching using digital technologies and includes the use of digital tools in education. Here again, the Numécole project was used to conduct extensive observations on digital learning. This programme included observations at

Toulon's underprivileged high schools and middle schools, study days with teachers, and a variety of digital incubator projects. The questions that emerged from these observations reflect the study's shifting focus from how digital tools are used to examining the specific interfaces from which these tools are accessed and interacted. Teachers participating in the Numécole experiment describe their professional uses of digital technology as word processing (90% of teachers), audiovisual documents (86%), web browsers (72%), teacher-created software or documents (69%), educational websites (62%), desktop publishing (49%), digital encyclopaedias (41%), online institutional resources (37%) and spreadsheets (18%), image and text edition (49%), and digital workspaces (43%).

The Numécole study also explored the motives and orientations that underpin the relationship between digital devices and teaching. Generally speaking, teachers' pedagogical practices are rather disciplinary (75%), although they indicate that they address cross-curricular methodological skills as soon as feasible (74%). Their biggest teaching challenge is student autonomy (77%). Individual and differentiated work prevail (77% and 56%) in classrooms where autonomous students are preferred (82%). The majority of participants also reported that they preferred to have student desks facing a blackboard (53%). Given this context, survey teachers declared that their main goals for using digital technology in the classroom were, in descending order of frequency: pedagogical differentiation, individualisation of learning, motivation, gamification, media variation (colours), test preparation, and media and information education.

We offer a critical method for studying the transformations caused by new educational media and digital mediations linked to new technologies. Digital acculturation helps us evaluate the emotive, psycho-cognitive, and pragmatic changes (Collet et al., 2021) of teachers and students facing mechanisation (Moeglin, 1993) and the rationalisation of learning that might be revived through the use of AI. Numécole instructors have proposed several ways to include ICT in instruction. These include the didactic approach, knowledge transmission, cognitive approach (80% of respondents ranked it first or second), school as intelligence development, the citizenship approach (school as a place of socialisation), the cultural approach (school as a place of cultural integration), and the professional approach (school as a place to prepare for professional integration).

## Digital Acculturation Within the Integration of Digital Technologies at School

We see acculturation as a paradigm for investigating the integration of digital technology in the classroom. Innovative programmes have been part of educational methods or dynamic initiatives, funded by the university, and present in teaching practices, for nearly 15 years. Students are stuck between contradicting injunctions and demands such as liberation, autonomy, individuation, involvement, commitment, support, and aid. They also include reintegration and accompaniment, which are seen as novel and stimulating dynamics provided by digital tools and technology.

We discovered in the Incubator programme that students saw school activities incorporating digital technology as an extension of their initiatives outside of the classroom. They continued to work in groups outside of class hours in order to develop transversal abilities. Knowing how to work as a team provided students with a higher level of autonomy, which is necessary for gaining subject-specific information. Across all observations, teachers stressed the contribution of digital tools in shaping the prevalent pedagogy by challenging routines and work habits and helping to break down existing barriers. Despite the time-consuming nature of technology, these tools permit the analysis of behavioural patterns and work habits and aid in decompartmentalisation.

Finally, digital acculturation is a concern of gaps between the usage and mastery of digital technology for both instructors and learners. It is also a question of the growth of the school form and, more widely, the educational environment, as well as a component of socio-cultural behaviours related with the usage of digital technologies (Kabuto & Harmey, 2019).

Digital acculturation is also the prospect of discovering new instructional strategies to involve students in techno creative activities (Romero et al., 2017). It is less about utilising technology and more about discovering how it may help create a deep knowledge of the United Nations' 2030 sustainability and development objectives jointly. In this regard, Faller and Heiser's (2022) CurriQvidéos device depicts several courses of action by first-time teachers who explain how digital tools (pedagogical robots, microcontrollers, etc.) and today's AI (using, for example, Google Teachable Machine, VittaScience, or 5J5IA) could be used to engage students in participatory activities that preserve natural and cultural heritage (Heiser et al., 2021). Finally, participating in the acculturation process implies an interest in the unstabilised evolution of education in reaction to, with, and by digital technology. This interaction is pedagogically led rather than assuming that the formation of digital citizenship would occur without deliberate involvement.

# Perspectives for Digital Acculturation with Regard to the Perspectives of AI in Learning and Education

In this section we explore how resources and perspectives associated with AI issues might challenge, redirect, or redefine the observed level of digital acculturation. Originally, a Médipath programme (Collet et al., 2021) outside of an educational context enabled us to measure the issues at stake during the reorientation of medical proficiencies linked to time savings and the facilitation of expertise. A programme within higher education and professional learning in the naval field (E-DEAL) envisages the modalities of transfer and acculturation to industrial digital practices gathered around the concepts of industry 4.0. Data management and the integration of AI are becoming training issues in their own right as a result of business transformations through the integration of these technologies. This research project also questions the representations and culture of industry players regarding the potential of AI and learning analytics (Lang et al., 2017; Siemens, 2013) in terms of profiling, individualisation of training paths, empowerment, and accentuation of self-learning practices for communities of learners in vocational training. Other insights emanating from special education show that, while digital technologies may crystallise tensions inherent in the field of social work, they are also able to support learners' performance, particularly in mathematics and reading (Bonjour & Daragon, 2019). This is significant given that many social workers find themselves unable to achieve these objectives. As such, AI offers support possibilities for cognitive and behavioural remediation for people with specific needs (Hopcan et al., 2022).

On the side of resources in educational platforms, questions oriented towards the evolution of organisational forms lead us to question the educational perspectives of AI. As educational platforms continue to incorporate AI technologies, there is an inherent need to reconsider how educators and learners adapt to and engage with the data generated by these tools. The challenges of AI in education seem to be oriented towards the identification of learning dynamics and contexts and the profiling, identification, and strategic construction of data, in order to initiate forms of learning centred on autonomy, self-training, and communities of learners in collaboration with teachers. These environments also establish the vision of a new performance of interfaces and mediations, supposedly experiential and efficient, in an approach that links the exploitation of artefacts, data, and new processes. We start from the challenges of translating AI into the ongoing digital acculturation with questions about the limits, constraints, and aporias in the education system or on forms of learning. It is then possible to consider AI as a break in continuity. Its integration into school or training environments still provokes speeches, debates, and past invocations, all of which find new vigour in the experiences and approaches related to AI and, at the same time, stimulate new issues or tensions at the heart of the world's education systems.

## References

Bellas, F., Guerreiro-Santalla, S., Naya, M., & Duro, R. J. (2023). AI curriculum for European high schools: An embedded intelligence approach. *International Journal of Artificial Intelligence in Education, 33*(2), 399–426.

Bernard, F., Beyaert-Geslin, A., Bouchardon, S., Bouillon, J.-L., Cerisier, J.-F., Chabert, G., Chaudiron, S., Damian-Gaillard, B., Douyère, D., Fleury, B., Galibert, O., Garcin-Marrou, I., Gimello-Mesplomb, F., Jacobi, D., Lafon, B., Legendre, B., Leleu-Merviel, S., Marchand, P., Marcon, C., & Zacklad, M. (2018). *Dynamique des recherches en sciences de l'information et de la communication.*

Bonfils, P. (2020). Repenser l'ingénierie pédagogique à l'aune de la pandémie? *Distances et médiations des savoirs* [En ligne], Rubrique Débats 31| 2020, mis en ligne le 16 octobre 2020.

Bonjour, A., & Daragon, E. (2019). *Information et données ouvertes: Un bien commun mis à mal dans les établissements et services sociaux et médico-sociaux?* Presses Universitaire de Nancy.

Brown, R., & Zagefka, H. (2011). The dynamics of acculturation: An intergroup perspective. In *Advances in experimental social psychology* (Vol. 44, pp. 129–184). Academic Press.

Collet, L., Durampart, M., Heiser, L., & Picard, L. (2021). Enjeux expérientiels de l'utilisation de l'IA en anatomopathologie. *Communiquer. Revue de communication sociale et publique, 33*, 26–44.

Durampart, M. (2016). La forme scolaire en action traversée par l'école numérique. *Revue française des sciences de l'information et de la communication* (9).

Faller, C., & Heiser, L. (2022). Croiser l'évaluation de compétences didactiques et numériques sur un même support: Un défi à relever dans un enregistrement vidéo (CurriQvidéo) en Master Enseignement Éducation et Formation du premier degré. *Médiations et médiatisations, 9*, 91–108.

Giraudon, G., Guitton, P., Romero, M., Roy, D., & Viéville, T. (2020). *Éducation et numérique, Défis et enjeux.* Inria.

Heiser, L., Faller, C., & Bonjour, A. (2021). *Rendre accessible, valoriser et préserver le patrimoine naturel et culturel via des pratiques technocréatives en enseignement moral et civique. Retour d'expérience du dispositif de formation des professeurs des écoles CurriqVidéo.* Axe 2 séminaire IMSIC.

Hopcan, S., Polat, E., Ozturk, M. E., & Ozturk, L. (2022). Artificial intelligence in special education: A systematic review. *Interactive Learning Environments, 31*(10), 1–19.

Kabuto, B., & Harmey, S. (2019). Literacy in a global context: Educational policy, pedagogy, and teacher education. *Global Education Review, 6*(2), 1–4.

Lang, C., Siemens, G., Wise, A., & Gasevic, D. (Eds.). (2017). *Handbook of learning analytics* (1st ed., p. 23). Society for Learning Analytics and Research (SoLAR).

Meyer, J. G., Urbanowicz, R. J., Martin, P. C., O'Connor, K., Li, R., Peng, P. C., & Moore, J. H. (2023). ChatGPT and large language models in academia: Opportunities and challenges. *BioData Mining, 16*(1), 20.

Moeglin, P. (1993). Le paradigme de la machine à enseigner. *Études de communication. langages, information, médiations*, (14), 103-91.

Pélissier, M., Dechamp, G., & Romero, M. (2018). *Le tournant créatif à l'université: Quelles modalités? Quels enjeux? Quelles légitimités?* https://archivesic.ccsd.cnrs.fr/sic_01823990

Pélissier, M., Pérocheau, G., Siarheyeva, A. A., & Collet, L. (2013). *Cultures numériques et trajectoires d'insertion professionnelle chez les 16-24 ans.* Enquête ObTIC. Université de Toulon.

Romero, M., Lille, B., & Patiño, A. (2017). *Usages créatifs du numérique pour l'apprentissage au XXIe siècle.* PUQ.

Siemens, G. (2013). Learning analytics: The emergence of a discipline. *American Behavioral Scientist, 57*(10), 1380–1400.

Vassilakopoulou, P., & Hustad, E. (2023). Bridging digital divides: A literature review and research agenda for information systems research. *Information Systems Frontiers, 25*(3), 955–969.

**Open Access** This chapter is licensed under the terms of the Creative Commons Attribution 4.0 International License (http://creativecommons.org/licenses/by/4.0/), which permits use, sharing, adaptation, distribution and reproduction in any medium or format, as long as you give appropriate credit to the original author(s) and the source, provide a link to the Creative Commons license and indicate if changes were made.

The images or other third party material in this chapter are included in the chapter's Creative Commons license, unless indicated otherwise in a credit line to the material. If material is not included in the chapter's Creative Commons license and your intended use is not permitted by statutory regulation or exceeds the permitted use, you will need to obtain permission directly from the copyright holder.

# 5

# Citizenship, Censorship, and Democracy in the Age of Artificial Intelligence

Tetiana Matusevych, Margarida Romero, and Oksana Strutynska

**Abstract** This chapter delves into the ethical dilemmas that arise from the incorporation of artificial intelligence (AI) into the field of education. It emphasises the importance of media literacy, AI literacy, and critical use of digital technologies in order to combat information conflicts, political manipulation, and AI inequality, among other issues. Potential threats to citizenship, such as AI censorship and disinformation, are examined in this chapter. Discourse is devoted to the dangers of deepfake technology as it pertains to the dissemination of false information and the manipulation of public sentiment; the significance of comprehending AI fundamentals and enforcing ethical standards is underscored.

---

T. Matusevych (✉) · O. Strutynska
Dragomanov Ukrainian State University, Kyiv, Ukraine
e-mail: t.v.matusevych@udu.edu.ua

O. Strutynska
e-mail: o.v.strutynska@udu.edu.ua

M. Romero
Université Côte d'Azur, Nice, France
e-mail: margarida.romero@univ-cotedazur.fr; margarida.romero@unice.fr

Notwithstanding the potential hazards, this chapter acknowledges the prospective advantages of AI in the field of education, which encompass gamification and adaptive learning paths. The text culminates by emphasising the significance of AI acculturation in enabling individuals to comprehend the ethical intricacies and arrive at well-informed judgements regarding the impact of AI on democracy, education, and citizenship.

**Keywords** AI fundamentals · AI literacy · Digital competence · Citizenship · AI ethics · AI algorithms

## Introduction

The rapid development of digital technologies and their widespread adoption make it necessary to develop citizens' digital competence and to actively engage people in their responsible use (Alexandre et al., 2020). Important components of citizens' digital competence include artificial intelligence (AI) literacy, critical use of digital technologies, and media literacy. These literacies are required due to the threats of information wars, political manipulation, but also digital and AI inequality and divisions (Calvo et al., 2020). These issues highlight the need to engage modern youth in responsible digital citizenship, which is an important component of citizenship education.

One of the conceptual initiatives to overcome these challenges was the creation of the *Digital Citizenship Education program* by the Council of Europe (Committee of Ministers Council Europe, 2019), which aims to provide young people with innovative opportunities to develop the values, attitudes, skills, and knowledge necessary for every citizen to fully participate and fulfil their responsibilities in society. *Digital citizens* are defined by the Council of Europe as people who are able to use digital tools to create, consume, communicate, and interact positively and responsibly with others. Digital citizens understand and respect human rights, embrace diversity, and prioritise lifelong learning as a way of keeping pace with societal changes.

*Digital civic education* is a holistic approach that aims to develop the basic skills and knowledge needed in today's connected world, as well as to foster values and attitudes that will ensure their wise and meaningful use. The development, regulation, involvement, and use of AI in education are part of this approach. In particular, it states that AI, like any other tool, offers many opportunities, but also poses significant threats that require the consideration of human rights principles in the early stages of its application. Educators need to be aware of the strengths and weaknesses of AI in education in order to empower their digital civic education practices (Committee of Ministers Council Europe, 2019). In this regard, Artificial Intelligence for Social Good (AI4SG) is also an important concept for civic education, which is becoming increasingly popular in professional circles (Hager et al., 2019). Projects aimed at using AI for the social good range from applications to help the hungry, to combating natural disasters, game-theoretic models aimed at poaching prevention, online HIV education for homeless youth, prevention of gender-based violence, and psychological support for students. (Floridi et al., 2020).

But despite the fact that new initiatives are emerging every day, researchers note that there is still only a limited understanding of what constitutes AI 'for the social good'. The lack of a clear understanding of what makes AI socially useful in theory, or what can be described as AI4SG in practice, and how to replicate its initial successes from a policy perspective creates at least two major obstacles for developers: avoidable mistakes and missed opportunities. AI software is shaped by human values, which, if not carefully selected, can lead to 'good AI goes bad' scenarios (Floridi et al., 2020). Thus, the issues of the value component and ethical principles of AI use are becoming increasingly relevant.

In general, the ethical issues of AI development and application are the focus of many researchers and international institutions, which has led to the creation of numerous initiatives, committees, and institutes of AI ethics. The Montreal AI Ethics Institute (MAIEI) published a guideline including the norms for responsible AI research and use (Dilhac et al., 2018). The Montreal Declaration for a Responsible Development of Artificial Intelligence is founded upon a set of ethical principles centred on seven fundamental values: well-being, autonomy, justice, privacy, knowledge, democracy, and responsibility. As a result of the analysis, researchers identified 84 published sets of ethical principles for AI that coincide in five areas: transparency, fairness and honesty, harmlessness, responsibility, and confidentiality (Jobin et al., 2019).

## Current Problems in the Integration of AI into Education

Despite the extensive debate around the ethical use of AI, there are a number of problems that have not yet been solved. The main ones are as follows:

1. *The polymorphic nature of the ethics of using AI in education.* AI ethics raises a number of complex issues centred on data (e.g., consent and data privacy) and how this data is analysed (e.g., transparency and trust). It is clear, however, that the ethics of AI in education cannot be reduced to issues of data and computational approaches alone. Research into the ethics of data and computing for AI in education is necessary but not sufficient. The ethics of AI in education should also take into account the ethics of education (Holmes et al., 2022).
2. *Potential threats to fundamental rights and democracy.* The results produced by AI depend on how it is designed and the data it utilises. Both the design and the data may be intentionally or unintentionally biassed. For example, some important aspects of the problem may not be programmed into the algorithm or may be programmed to reflect and repeat structural biases (Borenstein & Howard, 2021). In addition, the use of numbers to represent complex social realities may carry risks of apparent simplicity (Holmes et al., 2022). Another significant threat to human rights is data bias, which can affect the training of large language models (LLM) and result in biassed models For example, if an educational institution has student performance data biassed towards a certain ethnic, gender, or socioeconomic group, the AI system can learn to favour students from that particular group (Manyika & Silberg, 2019; Roselli et al., 2019). A further example of gender bias, this time in neural network algorithms for image generation, is provided in the research by Nikolić and Jovičić (2023). When working with the visual generative AI

services *DALL-E 2* and *Stable Diffusion*, the researchers observed the types of images the neural networks produced, particularly in relation to the representation of women in STEM. Specifically, when using the prompts 'engineer', 'scientist', 'mathematician', or 'IT expert', between 75 and 100% of the AI-generated images featured men, reinforcing stereotypes about male-dominated STEM professions: both as occupations that primarily attract men and as professions where men are prominent compared to women (Nikolić & Jovičić, 2023).

3. *AI colonialism in education.* AI colonialism can be understood in relation to the 'control, domination, and manipulation of human values' (Faruque, 2022, para. 25). AI colonialism is developed under an industrial perspective in which the business applications of AI are moved forward mainly for commercial objectives instead of humanistic ones. In 2020, in spite of the coronavirus pandemic, venture capital investment in AI startups reached US$75 billion for the year, of which about US$2 billion was invested in AI in education companies, predominantly based in the US. It is these companies that sell their interpretations around the world, creating what is called the colonialism of AI in education. This problem makes addressing cultural diversity one of the most challenging topics in AI in education (Blanchard, 2015). We can also consider the use of the English language as a form of colonialism in technology, given that it is the default language of consumption as well as the academic language in which AI specifications, frameworks, and ethical guidelines are produced and debated. Given that language not only conveys a symbolic representation of society, but also a cultural perspective of a certain context, we should acknowledge that having a default language reduces cultural perspectives and creates an accessibility challenge for those lacking the requisite language skills.

4. *Lack of a universal approach to regulating the ethical issues of using AI in education.* Unlike healthcare, where there are long-established ethical principles and codes of conduct for the treatment of humans, education (outside of university research) does not have the same universal approach or a commonly accepted model for ethics committees (Holmes et al., 2022). As such, when it comes to the

use of AI in education, most discussions treat students as data subjects rather than human beings. The learner activity is quantified in a way that reduces the representation of the learner into a quantitative model, mostly based on certain learning analytics. As a result, commercial players and schools may involve children in AI-driven systems without any ethical or other risk assessment (Holmes et al., 2022). In Europe, the AI Act (Pagallo et al., 2022) aims to advance the regulation of AI systems with the goal of making them 'safe, transparent, traceable, non-discriminatory, and environmentally friendly' (EU AI Act, 2023). Meanwhile, other countries are developing their own initiatives independently, without joint cooperation on a universal approach to AI regulation.

5. *Challenges of 'ethics washing'*. A large number of commercial actors in the tech sector publish ethics guidelines to 'wash away' concerns regarding their policies. This increasing instrumentalization of ethical guidelines by technology companies is called 'ethics washing' and refers to a situation where ethics is used by companies as an acceptable facade to justify deregulation, self-regulation, or market-driven governance, and is increasingly identified with the self-serving use and pretence of ethical behaviour (Bietti, 2020; van Maanen, 2022). For AI in education, given that children are the primary users of these commercial AI technologies, it is important to develop and implement robust ethical guidelines and avoid any 'ethics washing' (OECD, 2021).

6. *Lack of systematic application of ethical principles for the use of AI*. Although universities usually have robust research ethics procedures, most university or commercial AI research companies do not oversee AI ethics. This may be partly due to the fact that, in the early days of AI, research using human data was considered minimally risky (Holmes et al., 2022). The way AI is integrated into educational academic activities is regulated at different levels, including in schools or research labs, university and school departments, and government bodies such as the Ministries of Education of individual countries, all of whom may have different policies related to the ethical principles of AI. We should also consider that the end-user may not be able to evaluate the ethical principles of AI technologies,

meaning that AI creators have a responsibility to design and deploy AI technologies that recognise the varied ethical principles found in different national and professional domains.

7. *Threats of excessive and unjustified use of AI.* Overuse of AI can be problematic. Examples include investing in AI applications that turn out to be ineffective or applying AI to tasks for which it is not suited, such as explaining complex societal problems (Holmes et al., 2022). Automation of certain human activities related to education necessitates a high degree of sensitivity in determining what is appropriate, rather than merely what is possible. For example, it is important to continue to learn foreign languages even if automatic translations are available. Not only because human-to-human interaction is more empathetic, but also because there is a potential cognitive decline if we are not engaging in effortful cognitive activities such as learning, speaking, or writing in foreign languages. Finally, when evaluating the applications of AI, it is important to consider the energy consumption associated with its use versus alternative information search processes that may be less energy-intensive (Yang et al., 2021).

8. *Challenges of accountability and responsibility.* For educational institutions, the question is not only whether AI can be used in children's education, but also how accountability and responsibility should be determined when educators decide to adopt or reject any systemic recommendation (Holmes et al., 2022).

9. *Challenges of conflict of interest or 'AI loyalty'.* The concept of conflict of interest, or 'AI loyalty' (Aguirre et al., 2021) in educational institutions is largely absent in the current body of literature. For whom do AI systems work? Is it the students, schools, the education system, commercial players (e.g., AI edtech companies), or politicians? The question is not necessarily about the ethics of the technology itself, but rather about the ethics of the decision makers leading the companies behind AI's development, implementation, and use (Holmes et al., 2022). Understanding AI loyalty means clearly defining ownership and any conflicts of interest. To increase the transparency and credibility of AI applications, system developers and controllers should be required to clearly align the loyalty

of their AI systems and governance structures with the interests of learners and other stakeholders of their systems (Holmes et al., 2022). In their daily work, educators should be acculturated to the fundamentals of AI in order to decide which of its uses are relevant for the teaching or learning process, but also to be able to decline the use of certain AI technologies that are not relevant to their teaching practices.

10. *Decreased social connection and overreliance on technology.* There is a risk that an increase in time spent using AI systems will lead to a decrease in the interactions between students, teachers, and classmates. Kids might also begin substituting other human interactions (e.g., conversions with families and friends) with conversational AI systems amplifying and exacerbating the public health crises of loneliness, isolation, and disconnection (Bailey, 2023).

11. *AI threats to citizenship.* Widespread threats, such as AI censorship and AI misinformation, can lead to the manipulation of public opinion, contribute to the incitement of conflicts on various grounds (e.g., racial, religious, etc.), and contribute to the worsening of existing inequalities and stereotypes (e.g., gender inequalities). Filgueiras (2022) highlights the risks of AI in the context of authoritarianism in developing countries, which can amplify surveillance mechanisms put in place to control citizens considered a threat to the current establishment.

12. *AI censorship.* Due to the rapid development of AI, the threat of AI censorship has been added to internet censorship and the deletion of uncomfortable content practices (i.e., for political elites who want to influence public opinion). Censorship of political content on Chinese and Russian social media (e.g., active deletion of messages posted by individuals) is already having a corresponding impact on public opinion in these countries (Bamman et al., 2012; Ermoshina et al., 2022; Yang, 2016). Furthermore, AI censorship can dramatically affect the objectivity of people's perceptions of information. For example, motivated groups can adjust the algorithms of AI systems in such a way that inconvenient facts are hidden from the general public. The research on setting censorship parameters in neural networks and AI services by Ermoshina (2023) is an example of this

type of manipulation. Another example of this type of manipulation can be found in the Russian neural network Kandinsky 2.1, which returns images of flowers when given prompts of 'war in Ukraine', 'Ukrainian Flag', or even just the word 'Ukrainian' whether entered in Russian or English. This censorship is also present in the visual generative AI services of other countries: Chinese *ERNIE-ViLG*, American *DALL-E 2, Stable Diffusion, Midjourney* (Ermoshina, 2023).

13. *AI misinformation.* One of the biggest AI threats is disinformation and the potential of AI systems to generate massive amounts of propaganda. Dishonest groups can use these manipulations to incite hatred on a variety of grounds (e.g., racial, religious, etc.), to hurt people's feelings, and to arouse anger and other unpleasant emotions. An example of such disinformation can be found in the recent blog post exposing AI-generated fake images of violence in Gaza and Israel (Gault, 2023).

    One strategy for influencing public opinion and spreading misinformation or panic among populations is the creation and distribution of fake videos using deepfake technology. Deepfake is an AI-based method of generating fabricated images and videos by combining and superimposing images or videos onto other images or videos out of context (Sharma & Kaur, 2022). Often, this technology is used to discredit a person or for purposes of revenge. Deepfake videos regarding the war in Ukraine are examples of attempts to sow panic among the Ukrainian population with one example showing Ukrainian President Volodymyr Zelensky issuing a fabricated statement calling for the end of resistance to Russian aggressions (Rayon, 2022). Another recent example of such manipulations is a deepfake of the Commander-in-Chief of the Armed Forces of Ukraine, Valeriy Zaluzhny, calling for a coup d'état against the President of Ukraine (Espreso, 2023). Other examples of deepfake manipulations include the creation of nude images of Spanish schoolgirls highlighting an alarming trend among younger users. In this particular instance, a group of mothers, refusing to tolerate such exploitation, targeted not only the company responsible for creating the images, but also appealed to educational authorities to highlight the severe impact such images can have on the affected teenagers. The use of deepfakes poses a significant challenge to the epistemic trust undermining the reliability and importance of social communication (Twomey et al., 2023).

## Discussion

We have addressed in this chapter the different threats of AI in relation to citizenship, democracy, and censorship. Part of the challenges arising in the ethical use of AI in education require a better understanding of AI fundamentals. The understanding of data (i.e., collection and management), but also the way algorithms work, is important for ensuring that teachers and learners can develop their work from a critical thinking perspective.

AI, like any other tool, offers many opportunities, but also poses many threats that require the consideration of human rights principles at the earliest stages of its implementation. Educators should be aware of the strengths and weaknesses of AI in education to empower their digital, civic education practices. In particular, AI services and tools can be used to design adaptive learning paths, recommend resources, and offer scaffolding and other forms of assistance (e.g., to assign different levels of complexity, interaction, and differentiation). AI can also support the gamification of learning through the creation of engaging and interactive scenarios, challenges, and simulations that promote problem solving, critical thinking, creativity, collaboration, and digital literacy or citizenship. Furthermore, AI-based 'chatbots' can be developed for teachers and parents to support both the disciplinary and transversal aspects of education.

While AI can pose risks to citizenship when lacking an acculturation and regulation of its use, AI in education also provides advantages for both educators and learners by allowing them to avoid routine work and focus on creative tasks (Romero et al., 2021; Septiani et al., 2023). AI, through machine and deep learning, can enrich education and profoundly affect the interactions between teachers, students, and citizens at large. In this way, AI in education can promote free expression and independent and critical thinking through learning opportunities (Committee of Ministers Council Europe, 2019; Richardson & Milovidov, 2019).

According to Frąckiewicz (2023), the main areas of AI that can contribute to the development of education for responsible citizenship include: (i) developing the global dimension of responsible citizenship through the promotion of intercultural understanding; (ii) facilitating access to information and education; (iii) informed citizenship; (iv) democratisation of education, making it more accessible to students; and (v) the development of digital literacy skills. By developing digital literacy, AI can help students become responsible consumers of information and active participants in online discussions (Frąckiewicz, 2023).

The potential of AI for improving or harming citizenship and education will depend on the way citizens and governments decide to use and regulate it. An acculturation to the fundamentals of AI is required for each citizen to move beyond the role of mere 'consumer' of technology while also developing a critical, yet creative, perspective on its impact related to citizenship, well-being, education, and democracy.

# References

Aguirre, A., Reiner, P. B., Surden, H., & Dempsey, G. (2021). AI loyalty by design: A framework for governance of AI. In J. B. Bullock & others (Eds.), *The Oxford handbook of AI governance.* Available at SSRN Scholarly Paper 3930338. https://papers.ssrn.com/abstract=3930338

Alexandre, F., de Barretin, R., Becker, J., Comte, M.-H., Courbin, M., Cruchon, S., Lagarrigue, A., Masse, B., De Quatrebarbes, S., Stein, J., Terosier, C., & Vieville, T. (2020). *Understanding intelligently artificial intelligence: A citizens' open formation.* International Workshop on Education in Artificial Intelligence K-12 (EDUAI-20).

Bailey, J. (2023, Серпень 8). AI in education. *Education Next, 23*(4), 28–35. https://www.educationnext.org/a-i-in-education-leap-into-new-era-machine-intelligence-carries-risks-challenges-promises/

Bamman, D., O'Connor, B., & Smith, N. (2012). Censorship and deletion practices in Chinese social media. *First Monday*. https://doi.org/10.5210/fm.v17i3.3943

Bietti, E. (2020). From ethics washing to ethics bashing: A view on tech ethics from within moral philosophy. In *Proceedings of the 2020 conference on fairness, accountability, and transparency* (pp. 210–219). Association for Computing Machinery. https://doi.org/10.1145/3351095.3372860

Blanchard, E. G. (2015). Socio-cultural imbalances in AIED research: Investigations, implications and opportunities. *International Journal of Artificial Intelligence in Education, 25*(2), 204–228. https://doi.org/10.1007/s40593-014-0027-7

Borenstein, J., & Howard, A. (2021). Emerging challenges in AI and the need for AI ethics education. *AI and Ethics, 1*(1), 61–65. https://doi.org/10.1007/s43681-020-00002-7

Calvo, D., Cano-Orón, L., & Abengozar, A. E. (2020). Materials and assessment of literacy level for the recognition of social bots in political misinformation contexts. *ICONO 14, Revista de comunicación y tecnologías emergentes, 18*(2), 111–136.

Committee of Ministers Council Europe. (2019). *Recommendation CM/Rec(2019)10 of the Committee of Ministers to member States on developing and promoting digital citizenship education*. https://rm.coe.int/090000168098de08

Dilhac, M. A., Christophe, A., & Lehoux, P. (2018). *La Déclaration de Montréal IA responsable*. https://declarationmontreal-iaresponsable.com/la-declaration/

Ermoshina, K. (2023, Червень 15). *Украина, протесты и сексизм. Ксения Ермошина—О цензуре в нейросетях* (Ukraine, protests and sexism. Ksenia Yermoshina—On censorship in neural networks). Теплица социальных технологий. https://te-st.org/2023/06/15/ai-censorship/

Ermoshina, K., Loveluck, B., & Musiani, F. (2022). A market of black boxes: The political economy of Internet surveillance and censorship in Russia. *Journal of Information Technology & Politics, 19*(1), 18–33. https://doi.org/10.1080/19331681.2021.1905972

Espreso. (2023, Листопад 7). *Мережею шириться діпфейк із нібито Залужним і закликом до збройного повстання* (Dipfake with allegedly Zaluzhnyi and a call for armed rebellion spreads online) [News website]. Espreso. https://espreso.tv/merezheyu-shiritsya-dipfeyk-iz-nibito-zaluzhnim-i-zaklikom-do-zbroynogo-povstannya

European Parliament. (2023, August 6). *EU AI Act: First regulation on artificial intelligence*. https://www.europarl.europa.eu/news/en/headlines/society/20230601STO93804/eu-ai-act-first-regulation-on-artificial-intelligence

Faruque, M. U. (2022). AI versus human consciousness: A future with machines as our masters? *Renovatio: The Journal of Zaytuna College*. https://renovatio.zaytuna.edu/article/ai-versus-human-consciousness

Filgueiras, F. (2022). The politics of AI: Democracy and authoritarianism in developing countries. *Journal of Information Technology & Politics, 19*(4), 449–464. https://doi.org/10.1080/19331681.2021.2016543

Floridi, L., Cowls, J., King, T. C., & Taddeo, M. (2020). How to design AI for social good: Seven essential factors. *Science and Engineering Ethics, 26*(3), 1771–1796. https://doi.org/10.1007/s11948-020-00213-5

Frąckiewicz, M. (2023, May 4). *The role of AI in fostering global citizenship education*. TS2 SPACE. https://ts2.space/en/the-role-of-ai-in-fostering-global-citizenship-education/

Gault, M. (2023, November 7). *Adobe Is selling AI-generated images of violence in Gaza and Israel*. Vice. https://www.vice.com/en/article/3akj3k/adobe-is-selling-fake-ai-generated-images-of-violence-in-gaza-and-israel

Hager, G. D., Drobnis, A., Fang, F., Ghani, R., Greenwald, A., Lyons, T., Parkes, D. C., Schultz, J., Saria, S., Smith, S. F., & Tambe, M. (2019). *Artificial intelligence for social good* (arXiv:1901.05406). arXiv. https://doi.org/10.48550/arXiv.1901.05406

Holmes, W., Persson, J., Chounta, I.-A., Wasson, B., & Dimitrova, V. (2022). *Artificial intelligence and education: A critical view through the lens of human rights, democracy and the rule of law*. Council of Europe.

Jobin, A., Ienca, M., & Vayena, E. (2019). The global landscape of AI ethics guidelines. *Nature Machine Intelligence, 1*(9), 389–399. https://doi.org/10.1038/s42256-019-0088-2

Manyika, J., & Silberg, J. (2019, June). *Notes from the AI frontier: Tackling bias in AI (and in humans)*. Multidisciplinary symposium on ethics in AI hosted by DeepMind Ethics and Society. https://www.mckinsey.com/~/media/McKinsey/Featured%20Insights/Artificial%20Intelligence/Tackling%20bias%20in%20artificial%20intelligence%20and%20in%20humans/MGI-Tackling-bias-in-AI-June-2019.pdf

Nikolić, K., & Jovičić, J. (2023, April 3). *Reproducing inequality: How AI image generators show biases against women in STEM*. UNDP. https://www.undp.org/serbia/blog/reproducing-inequality-how-ai-image-generators-show-biases-against-women-stem

OECD. (2021). *OECD digital education outlook 2021: Pushing the frontiers with artificial intelligence, blockchain and robots.* Organisation for Economic Co-operation and Development. https://www.oecd-ilibrary.org/education/oecd-digital-education-outlook-2021_589b283f-en

Pagallo, U., Ciani Sciolla, J., & Durante, M. (2022). The environmental challenges of AI in EU law: Lessons learned from the Artificial Intelligence Act (AIA) with its drawbacks. *Transforming Government: People, Process and Policy, 16*(3), 359–376. https://doi.org/10.1108/TG-07-2021-0121

Rayon. (2022, Березень 17). *Компанія Meta видалила діпфейк із Зеленським* (Meta deletes Zelenskyy's diplomatic account). Rayon. https://rayon.in.ua/news/498190-kompaniya-meta-vidalila-dipfeyk-iz-zelenskim

Richardson, J., & Milovidov, E. (2019). *Digital citizenship education handbook: Being online, well-being online, rights online.* Council of Europe.

Romero, M., Heiser, L., & Galindo, L. (2021). *L'intelligence artificielle en éducation, formation/acculturation et modélisation.* https://hal.science/hal-03195064

Roselli, D., Matthews, J., & Talagala, N. (2019). *Managing bias in AI*. Paper Presented at the Companion Proceedings of The 2019 World Wide Web Conference, 539–544. https://doi.org/10.1145/3308560.3317590

Septiani, D. P., Kostakos, P., & Romero, M. (2023). Analysis of creative engagement in AI tools in education based on the #PPai6 framework. In B Z. Kubincová, F. Caruso, T. Kim, M. Ivanova, L. Lancia, & M. A. Pellegrino (Eds.). *Methodologies and intelligent systems for technology enhanced learning, workshops—13th international conference* (Vol. 769, pp. 48–58). Springer. https://doi.org/10.1007/978-3-031-42134-1_5

Sharma, M., & Kaur, M. (2022). A review of deepfake technology: An emerging AI threat. In B G. Ranganathan, X. Fernando, F. Shi, & Y. El Allioui (Eds.), *Soft computing for security applications* (pp. 605–619). Springer. https://doi.org/10.1007/978-981-16-5301-8_44

Twomey, J., Ching, D., Aylett, M. P., Quayle, M., Linehan, C., & Murphy, G. (2023). Do deepfake videos undermine our epistemic trust? A thematic analysis of tweets that discuss deepfakes in the Russian invasion of Ukraine. *PLoS ONE, 18*(10), e0291668. https://doi.org/10.1371/journal.pone.0291668

van Maanen, G. (2022). AI ethics, ethics washing, and the need to politicize data ethics. *Digital Society, 1*(2). https://go.gale.com/ps/i.do?p=AONE&sw=w&issn=27314669&v=2.1&it=r&id=GALE%7CA712345544&sid=googleScholar&linkaccess=abs

Yang, F. (2016). Rethinking China's Internet censorship: The practice of recording and the politics of visibility. *New Media & Society, 18*(7), 1364–1381. https://doi.org/10.1177/1461444814555951

Yang, S. J. H., Ogata, H., Matsui, T., & Chen, N.-S. (2021). Human-centered artificial intelligence in education: Seeing the invisible through the visible. *Computers and Education: Artificial Intelligence, 2*, 100008. https://doi.org/10.1016/j.caeai.2021.100008

**Open Access** This chapter is licensed under the terms of the Creative Commons Attribution 4.0 International License (http://creativecommons.org/licenses/by/4.0/), which permits use, sharing, adaptation, distribution and reproduction in any medium or format, as long as you give appropriate credit to the original author(s) and the source, provide a link to the Creative Commons license and indicate if changes were made.

The images or other third party material in this chapter are included in the chapter's Creative Commons license, unless indicated otherwise in a credit line to the material. If material is not included in the chapter's Creative Commons license and your intended use is not permitted by statutory regulation or exceeds the permitted use, you will need to obtain permission directly from the copyright holder.

# Part II

## Artificial Intelligence in K-12 Education

# 6

# International Initiatives and Regional Ecosystems for Supporting Artificial Intelligence Acculturation

Margarida Romero, Isabelle Galy, Jérémy Camponovo, Florence Tressols, and Alex Urmeneta

**Abstract** National and international initiatives to support AI education are discussed in this chapter. Following an examination of the various initiatives undertaken in OECD countries, the chapter highlights the House of Artificial Intelligence (MIA) activities supporting AI acculturation to the regional educational and industrial ecosystem in the French Rivera. The chapter delves into these achievements, detailing partnerships, educational outreach, entrepreneurship initiatives,

---

M. Romero (✉) · F. Tressols · A. Urmeneta
Université Côte d'Azur, Nice, France
e-mail: margarida.romero@univ-cotedazur.fr; margarida.romero@unice.fr

A. Urmeneta
e-mail: alex.urmeneta@etu.univ-cotedazur.fr

I. Galy
Maison de l'Intelligence Artificielle, Biot, France
e-mail: IGALY@maison-intelligence-artificielle.com

J. Camponovo
DANE, Nice, France
e-mail: Jeremy.Camponovo@ac-nice.fr

© The Author(s) 2024
A. Urmeneta and M. Romero (eds.), *Creative Applications of Artificial Intelligence in Education*, Palgrave Studies in Creativity and Culture,
https://doi.org/10.1007/978-3-031-55272-4_6

and the nuanced approach to addressing gender biases in AI education. Through the different workshops, students are empowered to actively contribute to AI's evolution, transforming from consumers to creators. Gender perspectives are explored, tackling stereotypes and biases. The chapter concludes with a spotlight on the Smart Hive project, an interdisciplinary initiative fostering sustainable development through AI, exemplifying the MIA's role in creating a regional ecosystem for AI acculturation.

**Keywords** AI education · AI acculturation · Hackathon · Gender · Entrepreneurship

## Introduction

As artificial intelligence (AI) technologies become more common in many areas of civic life, helping people of all ages become more comfortable with AI is becoming an important part of being a critical and active citizen (Alexandre et al., 2021). The necessity of providing all citizens with the knowledge and critical thinking skills necessary to actively engage as informed and discerning agents in a societal landscape where AI advancements are permeating is what gives acculturation to AI its importance. In line with the broader goal of acculturating citizens to AI, there are initiatives such as Terra Numerica and the *Maison de l'Intelligence Artificielle* (MIA), the "house" of AI, in Sophia Antipolis in France.

Different OECD countries have developed initiatives oriented toward the general public, including massive open online courses (MOOCs), outreach activities at different moments of the year, and also activities such as expositions. To identify the different initiatives, the OECD.ai repository integrates an important number of initiatives at the governmental level, financial support, and organizations. Among these initiatives, some OECD countries have specifically addressed citizen acculturation, formal education, and information education. OECD.AI serves as a global hub for AI policy, offering freely accessible tools and resources to all stakeholders. With a focus on AI risks, accountability, potential futures, incident tracking, and the environmental impact of AI, it collaboratively engages a diverse network of over 250 experts to inform policy responses and create a comprehensive platform for AI policymakers worldwide.

At the school level, different initiatives have emerged in the last few years to support the introduction of AI fundamentals to learners in primary and secondary education. These initiatives sometimes emerge from the teachers' initiative, but in other cases, they are promoted through Ministry of Education initiatives. The review of Schiff (2022) identified 30 countries that have issued national artificial intelligence (AI) policy strategies outlining plans and expectations for AI's. He evaluates 24 of these strategies concerning the educational sector. Schiff (2022) observes that discussions regarding the use of AI in education are mostly instrumental, focused on developing an AI-ready workforce instead of considering AI's ethical and societal impact.

In 2023, the National Artificial Intelligence (AI) Strategy and the EdTech Masterplan 2030, as outlined by the Singaporean Ministry of Education (MOE), advocated for the integration of an adaptive learning system to support mathematics education. The system will also feature a Language Feedback Assistant for English to support the learning process by allowing the teacher to focus on the complex tasks and activities associated with teaching. In India, the "AI for All" initiative proposes an online program for citizens with the goal of demystify AI. The U.S. Department of Education Office of Educational Technology's recent policy report, "Artificial Intelligence and the Future of Teaching and Learning: Insights and Recommendations" (Cardona et al., 2023) emphasizes the imperative to disseminate knowledge, involve educators, and enhance technology plans and policies regarding AI in education. The report defines AI as a swiftly advancing technology for pattern recognition and automation, guiding educators on how to leverage these technologies to achieve educational objectives while assessing and mitigating any associated risks.

At the university level, initiatives such as EFELIA, or the "Ecole Française de l'IA" (French School of AI), have facilitated the development of student accessible courses to support the development of AI fundamentals across various domains. The modules cover AI's role in the humanities, linguistics, and social sciences emphasizing image and text analysis. Additionally, the program explores AI's impact on cultural and creative industries, its role in applied foreign languages, and its applications within healthcare ecosystems and biology. The EFELIA course delves into the intersection of AI with law, administration, and public service, addressing the associated challenges of AI's use in these disciplines. A specific course on AI for school teachers spans primary, middle, and secondary education levels, offering insights into integrating AI into educational practices. The series also includes a module focused on AI in adult education, reflecting the diverse applications and implications of AI across various use cases.

In the European context, outreach initiatives to facilitate the acculturation of citizens to artificial intelligence (AI) encompass a multifaceted approach. Educational workshops and training programs conduct hands-on sessions across cities, enabling citizens to actively engage with AI applications and participate in discussions emphasizing responsible AI use. Public awareness campaigns, such as the European Commission's "AI Watch"[1] utilize social media platforms to disseminate information about ongoing AI developments and share the AI policies of different European countries. Community engagement events, like AI meetups, provide forums for citizens to interact with local AI experts, fostering dialogues on AI's impact on daily life. Online platforms, exemplified by the website "AI4Good"[2], offer easily accessible resources, including videos and articles, to demystify AI concepts and broaden citizens' understanding. Partnerships between AI industry leaders and educational institutions result in AI-focused educational programs, ensuring students are equipped with essential AI knowledge. In France, the PIA program, supported by the Ministry of Education, has supported companies such as EvidenceB to develop math (*AdaptivMaths*[3]) and language learning platforms (*AdaptivLangue*)[4] integrating AI technologies. Initiatives such as AI hackathons encourage citizens to collaboratively develop

---

[1] https://ai-watch.ec.europa.eu/.
[2] https://ai4good.org/.
[3] https://www.evidenceb.fr/produits/adaptiv-math.
[4] https://www.evidenceb.fr/produits/adaptiv-langue.

AI solutions addressing societal challenges, promoting creativity and developing problem-solving skills. Policy advocacy forums, such as the AI Observatory (OBVIA[5]) create spaces for policymakers, industry leaders, and citizens to collaboratively shape AI policies based on public input. Collaborations with NGOs ensure a diverse range of voices are included in AI discussions, emphasizing societal impacts and ethical considerations. Multilingual outreach strategies, employed by the European AI Alliance,[6] ensure that information about AI is accessible to citizens across language barriers. Lastly, the European Commission's guidelines on the ethics of AI in education provides recommendations for educators and parents alike on responsible AI use in educational settings (European Commission, Directorate-General for Education, Youth, Sport and Culture, 2022). Collectively, these initiatives represent a proactive and diverse approach across Europe to engage citizens in understanding, discussing, and shaping the societal impact of AI.

## AI Acculturation in the House of Artificial Intelligence

Third places have the potential to facilitate a broad spectrum of AI activities. Developed with the goal of acculturating the general public to AI and serving as a hub for start-ups and upscaling initiatives, the Maison de l'Intelligence Artificielle (MIA) is an ambitious third-place project open to everyone. MIA's activities are inclusive, welcoming kindergarten to-high school aged learners, teachers, families, and professionals from diverse domains, with the overarching aim of fostering a deeper understanding of AI.

According to MIA director, Ms. Isabelle Galy, the primary concern associated with AI acculturation is the possible proliferation of misunderstandings among the younger participants. Specific AI educational activities use robots to illustrate AI concepts or emphasize algorithms and data. Instances where intelligence is personified in representations

---

[5] https://observatoire-ia.ulaval.ca/.
[6] https://digital-strategy.ec.europa.eu/en/policies/european-ai-alliance.

involving robotics frequently foster erroneous expectations regarding the capabilities of AI and frequently correspond with science fiction narratives. Likewise, an overemphasis on algorithms and data alone may result in overly digital illustrations, potentially blurring the distinction between digital tools and AI for learners. Such misrepresentation can create biases that will be difficult to rectify later in their education. In order to address this, it is critical to implement a multiperspective approach to AI acculturation. This strategy should incorporate machine learning methodologies and the computational modeling components of artificial intelligence across a range of AI technologies and use case illustrations. The purpose of this all-encompassing approach is to provide participants with a nuanced comprehension of AI and prevent the formation of erroneous perceptions.

One of the proposed activities at the MIA is the use of generative AI, exemplified by ChatGPT, which has proven effective in examining how AI forms a representation of the world through an encoder and how it reproduces the generated world through a decoder. This technology enables a multi-approach pedagogy based on definition, researcher works, technology, engineering, outcomes, and human understanding. An additional noteworthy aspect of the MIA is the exhibition of AI-focused companies. French industrial ecosystem start-ups and AI companies exhibit their technologies at these demonstrations, with an emphasis on the necessity to improve the comprehensibility of information for end-users. These showcases promote a dialogue-based comprehension of AI technologies developed by national companies among end-users (including professionals, students, and teachers) of diverse ages and backgrounds, thereby providing substantial advantages for both parties involved. The MIA benefits from a highly significant scientific and technological environment. The French Riviera is an AI hub, and AI-producing companies, research laboratories, and the 3IA create educational demonstrators to assist young learners in forming a genuine understanding of what AI is and to comprehend its importance in their studies of mathematics and language proficiency. Furthermore, this aspect highlights the possibility that organizations situated in various nations could create AI-driven technologies that are customized to meet particular cultural requirements.

Within the diverse array of activities offered, the Arc-en-ciel project (2020–2023), spearheaded by MIA, in collaboration with Université Côte d'Azur, Alpes-Maritimes Department, INRIA, Academie de Nice and CNRS, is dedicated to fostering awareness of artificial intelligence (AI) among middle school students in the French Riviera. This initiative encompasses four pivotal projects: educational activities at the MIA, school or extracurricular internships, addressing biases and gender stereotypes in AI, and activities conducted beyond the walls within the departmental territory. The chapter provides a comprehensive exploration of both the achievements and the extensive partnerships that facilitated them. Simultaneously, the SMART Deal project, managed by MIA in Sophia Antipolis is committed to supporting digital transformation. This initiative aims to raise AI awareness in middle school students over three years, emphasizing practical AI education, dispelling misconceptions, and offering mentorship to highlight potential study pathways and career opportunities in the field of AI. This chapter presents the achievements of the Arc-en-ciel project, including the organization of school and extracurricular internships, visits to the MIA by school groups, and scientific mediation activities carried out directly in French Rivera's middle schools. It also provides context around the founding of the project, describing the various partnerships and agreements that led to the opening of the MIA in 2020, its mission, and the collaborations it maintains with the Université Côte d'Azur, mainly on questions of teaching AI and gender equity, and through the collaboration of partners such as AlterEgaux.

## The Outreach Curriculum for the Acculturation to AI

The outreach curriculum for AI acculturation encompasses diverse activities, including AI use case demonstrations at the MIA, school visits, extracurricular internships, and training provided by the Regional Academic Delegation for Digital Education (DRANE) in collaboration with the MIA. The MIA mediation team, in consultation with grade-level teachers and the target audience, meticulously selects scientific and cultural activities. Prioritizing effective communication, the team considers primary and secondary messages, audience, AI techniques, required participants, and logistical details such as equipment weight should there be a need for transportation. Currently undergoing a trial and refinement phase, these activities aim to enhance effectiveness and broaden outreach. This approach highlights the project's dedication to tailoring AI education outreach to middle school students and teachers. Additionally, training was provided on-site to 30 teachers in collaboration with Terra Numerica. Another initiative, Teacher Wednesdays, supports in-service AI acculturation and allows teachers to explore diverse AI applications in education.

## Entrepreneurship in the Age of AI

The objective of this project is to equip students with entrepreneurial skills. Specifically, it seeks to develop student agency in an environment increasingly influenced by AI, enabling them to transform their environment (Engeström & Sannino, 2013). In this way, students assume the role of creators, innovating with digital technology and AI, rather than merely consuming AI tools. Students are encouraged to "take charge" with the understanding that they can actively contribute to AI's evolution by acknowledging interests, confronting fears or beliefs, and addressing any apprehensions about its foundational use. This approach also develops student representations (Ghotbi & Ho, 2021).

The "Entrepreneurship in the Age of AI" project, offered during the final year of middle school, includes observation and extracurricular internships. Observational internships pair participants with companies to observe AI use cases and explore potential career paths. Week-long extracurricular courses during holidays involve large-scale AI projects, incorporating kinesthetic experiments, unplugged algorithmic activities, and ideation challenges with design thinking principles. Participants tackle problems like "How can AI assist in sports?" or "How can AI contribute to managing energy consumption?" by creating empathy maps and prototypes using LEGO blocks or digital tools. The week concludes with student project presentations and jury evaluations, emphasizing perseverance, cooperation, and creativity.

## Gender Perspectives in the Acculturation to AI

The technology field, and AI in particular, is significantly impacted by gender stereotyping and bias (Franzoni, 2023; Marinucci et al., 2023). The Arc-en-ciel project acknowledges these challenges and aims to catalyze a transformation in attitudes and practices, concurrently increasing awareness among educators, mediation specialists, and students regarding the consequences of gender bias in AI. For instance, Norouzi et al. (2020) found that girls exhibited less confidence than boys in computer programming skills during an AI initiation project. In response to these persistent stereotypes, a collaboration between members of the French Rivera Diversity Club and the AlterEgaux organization initiated a project with three main objectives: creating a digital handbook, conducting studies on gender bias in mixed groups, and organizing intervention classes for International Women's Rights Day.

The digital handbook, a thirty-page guide, invites participants to identify gender stereotypes and question their prejudices through short educational activities. The second objective involved studies in partnership with the LINE lab at the Université Côte d'Azur and AlterEgaux. Data was collected through feedback mechanisms including student questionnaires, observations during mediation activities, and an interactive game titled "Diversity in AI professions" offered to participants of extracurricular internships. Preliminary findings noted boys' tendency to monopolize speech and attention in mixed groups, often at the expense of their female counterparts. A similar phenomenon was observed in other MIA interventions, accentuated by a lack of examples modeling gender equality, the absence of epicene language, and a dearth of female role models. Boys often positioned themselves at the front of the room, demonstrating a heightened interest in the subject matter even before sessions commenced. Facilitators also observed that their interventions had a more pronounced impact on boys' outcomes than on girls, regardless of the facilitator's gender.

The third objective involved classes organized by MIA, AlterEgaux, and the Women Hacker Action Tank (WHAT06) to discuss diversity in science and career pathways in digital and AI-integrated fields. Held in conjunction with International Women's Rights Day, these classes provided participants with the opportunity to meet inspiring female role models and engage in roundtable discussions focused on breaking down barriers for women in technology. These classes, and the meaningful connections they inspired, demonstrate that values such as cooperation, flexibility, perseverance, analysis, organization, creativity, leadership, and precision transcend gender boundaries.

## The Smart Hive Interdisciplinary Project

As part of the Fête de la Science celebration, MIA presented various activities, notably an AI hackathon aimed at crafting a smart hive. Dubbed the IAckathon, students actively participated in a design thinking approach to formulate an AI-based solution. The outcomes of this event, with involvement from college FabLabs responding to a call from the Regional Academic Directorate for Digital Education (DRANE), were showcased at the World AI Cannes Festival (Fig. 6.1).

The IAckathon aimed to execute an interdisciplinary project, seamlessly integrating AI while aligning with the sustainability objective. The theme of the intelligent hive was chosen for its promise to span various disciplines, extending beyond scientific subjects. Sustainable development was addressed through perspectives such as biodiversity preservation and resource conservation via edge computing (Shi et al., 2016). During the event, students from four Alpes-Maritimes middle schools made substantial contributions including participating in an interdisciplinary exploration of smart hives, where they collaborated closely with a beekeeper and conducted hands-on experiments with IoT sensors for data acquisition. Their activities included optimizing sensor placement, analyzing energy requirements, and exploring machine learning applications to enhance understanding of bee colony activities.

Fig. 6.1 World AI Cannes Festival

## A Regional Ecosystem for Supporting AI Acculturation

Establishing a regional ecosystem for fostering AI acculturation, the MIA actively collaborates with various stakeholders in scientific, technical, and industrial sectors. This collaborative approach allows stakeholders to share their perspectives, collectively raising awareness among students through local, national, and international initiatives. The overarching goal is to enhance the methods of educational mediation through this collaborative effort.

Over the past years, Terra Numerica and the MIA have undertaken educational interventions within the Arc-en-ciel project. These endeavors focus on highlighting the impact of AI use cases and providing the necessary resources and pedagogical training to demystify AI applications. Supported by institutional, academic, and industrial partners, these activities align with the MIA's comprehensive, multidisciplinary approach to AI. Themes like culture, territory, and daily life enhance use cases by grounding them in real-world scenarios. The Arc-en-ciel project, through its four initiatives, is committed to educating secondary school students in the Alpes-Maritimes department on the use and implications of AI. Further initiatives, including participation in events like the Science Festival and Brain Week, aim to move beyond school age students to enhance digital literacy for all residents of the department.

## Discussion

The dynamic landscape of AI acculturation shows different initiatives at the regional and international level. Among these initiatives, the House of Artificial Intelligence (MIA) is an important initiative in the acculturation of AI for a large number of stakeholders including students and their teachers, but also the AI industrial ecosystem. Projects such as 'Entrepreneurship in the Age of AI' and the IAhackatons serve to empower students not only as users of AI, but as active contributors to its transformative journey through interdisciplinary collaboration, sustainability goals, and the integration of AI into diverse citizenship challenges. The chapter concludes by underscoring the importance of regional ecosystems, emphasizing the MIA's collaborative efforts with Terra Numerica and other stakeholders, shaping an inclusive and enriching educational experience for students and promoting collaboration within the French Rivera's AI ecosystem. Within the different initiatives, we aim to highlight the gender perspectives, tackled through strategic projects and interventions, exemplify a commitment to fostering inclusivity, and dismantling biases in the AI domain. The continued consideration of the gender perspective should be stressed not only at regional levels but also at the international level to ensure the development of AI technologies that reduce gender bias and promote human–AI collaboration for a diverse group of users.

## References

Alexandre, F., Becker, J., Comte, M. H., Lagarrigue, A., Liblau, R., Romero, M., & Viéville, T. (2021). Why, what and how to help each citizen to understand artificial intelligence? *KI-Künstliche Intelligenz, 35*(2), 191–199.

Cardona, M. A., Rodríguez, R. J., & Ishmael, K. (2023). *Artificial intelligence and the future of teaching and learning*. Department of Education. https://tech.ed.gov/ai/

Engeström, Y., & Sannino, A. (2013). La volition et l'agentivité transformatrice: perspective théorique de l'activité. *Revue international du CRIRES: Innover dans la tradition de Vygotsky*.

European Commission, Directorate-General for Education, Youth, Sport and Culture. (2022). *Ethical guidelines on the use of artificial intelligence (AI) and data in teaching and learning for educators*. Publications Office of the European Union. https://data.europa.eu/doi/10.2766/153756

Franzoni, V. (2023). Gender differences and bias in artificial intelligence. In *Gender in AI and robotics: The gender challenges from an interdisciplinary perspective* (pp. 27–43). Springer.

Ghotbi, N., & Ho, M. T. (2021). Moral awareness of college students regarding artificial intelligence. *Asian Bioethics Review, 13*(4), 421–433.

Marinucci, L., Mazzuca, C., & Gangemi, A. (2023). Exposing implicit biases and stereotypes in human and artificial intelligence: State of the art and challenges with a focus on gender. *AI & Society, 38*(2), 747–761.

Norouzi, N., Chaturvedi, S., & Rutledge, M. (2020, April). Lessons learned from teaching machine learning and natural language processing to high school students. In *Proceedings of the AAAI conference on artificial intelligence* (Vol. 34, No. 09, pp. 13397–13403).

Schiff, D. (2022). Education for AI, not AI for education: The role of education and ethics in national AI policy strategies. *International Journal of Artificial Intelligence in Education, 32*(3), 527–563.

Shi, W., Cao, J., Zhang, Q., Li, Y., & Xu, L. (2016). Edge computing: Vision and challenges. *IEEE Internet of Things Journal, 3*(5), 637–646.

**Open Access** This chapter is licensed under the terms of the Creative Commons Attribution 4.0 International License (http://creativecommons.org/licenses/by/4.0/), which permits use, sharing, adaptation, distribution and reproduction in any medium or format, as long as you give appropriate credit to the original author(s) and the source, provide a link to the Creative Commons license and indicate if changes were made.

The images or other third party material in this chapter are included in the chapter's Creative Commons license, unless indicated otherwise in a credit line to the material. If material is not included in the chapter's Creative Commons license and your intended use is not permitted by statutory regulation or exceeds the permitted use, you will need to obtain permission directly from the copyright holder.

# 7

# Informal Education Practices for Human–AI Creative Pedagogy for Accessibility and Inclusivity

Caroline Boulord, Yann-Aël Le Borgne, and Patricia Corieri

**Abstract** The Scientotheque, a Brussels-based association committed to accessibility and inclusivity in technology for marginalised populations, addresses the challenge of integrating artificial intelligence (AI) into society with a focus on equity. This chapter outlines the association's educational initiatives since 2020, emphasising teacher training and AI workshops for disadvantaged youth. Through partnerships, the Scientotheque collaborates on diverse projects, promoting STEM skills and combating gender bias. The chapter details the association's educational approach to AI, employing project-based pedagogy and offering

C. Boulord (✉) · P. Corieri
Scientotheque, Brussels, Belgium
e-mail: caroline.boulord@gmail.com

P. Corieri
e-mail: corieri.patricia@ulb.be

Y.-A. Le Borgne
Free University of Brussels, Brussels, Belgium
e-mail: yannael@lascientotheque.be

a comprehensive catalog of over 200 educational resources. The Scientotheque prioritises teacher support, recognising the pivotal role of ongoing assistance. Activities conducted during the 2020–2021 school year demonstrate how the Scientotheque effectively engages young learners, demystifying complex AI concepts through hands-on, collaborative, and fun activities. The chapter concludes by highlighting the Scientotheque's pioneering role in AI education in Belgium and its involvement in the AI4InclusiveEducation project, aiming to provide inclusive AI education content.

**Keywords** AI education · Inclusive education · Citizenship · Diversity · Teacher education

## Introduction

A major challenge in the societal integration of artificial intelligence (AI) is the move towards greater inclusion of vulnerable populations and the equitable distribution of its potential benefits (Chauhan & Kshetri, 2022; Stypinska, 2023). This chapter presents the avenues explored in this direction by the Scientotheque, an association rooted in Brussels that has been working for 20 years to ensure the accessibility of new technologies to marginalised populations. This chapter describes the educational systems put in place since 2020 aimed at training teachers on the uses of AI in educational settings as well as feedback from AI workshops carried out with young people from disadvantaged backgrounds. Beyond the training and outreach activities described here, this chapter aims to illustrate the importance of the associative network in the creation of innovative educational resources and in the reduction of the digital divide (Kitsara, 2022).

## Equal Opportunity Through Science

The Scientotheque is a non-profit association based in the Experimentarium, Physics Museum of the Free University of Brussels. Two realities led to the establishment of the association: the increased risk of attrition and the limited accessibility to higher education for young people from precarious backgrounds (Coslin, 2012) and the underrepresentation of females in STEM-related subjects and careers. Considering that attracting girls to scientific or technological projects can prove challenging (Blanchard, 2021), the inclusion of AI-related activities in a school environment serves as a method of counteracting gender bias (Ahn et al., 2022; Sartori et al., 2023). Since its foundation in 2001, its primary mission has focused on reducing social inequalities.

The main objective of the association is to support young people aged 4–20 during school and extracurricular experimentation workshops where science, technology, engineering, arts, and mathematics (STEAM) come together in a multidisciplinary approach. With this objective in mind, the Scientotheque also provides pedagogical training to teachers and support staff on the integration of digital tools within academic environments. More recently, the COVID health crisis has had a "magnifying effect" on social inequalities, and therefore on the phenomenon of the "digital divide" (Fenoglio, 2021; Lucas, 2020). In response to the growing importance of digital literacy, the Scientotheque has prioritised digital activities, which have become a central component in the workshops and initiatives conducted by the library.

The motto of the Scientotheque is "equal opportunity through science". This specificity is intentional and aligns with the association's mission of promoting STEAM activities and fighting against social, cultural and gender discrimination in schools. The approach of the Scientotheque consists of fighting against school attrition and social inequalities, the two being linked, by offering STEAM activities to young people utilising a multidisciplinary approach.

With the growth of its expertise and the increasing visibility of its projects, the Scientotheque has frequently been called upon by education professionals, including teachers and association actors in

Brussels, seeking the organisation's leadership in conducting STEAM[1] workshops, developing educational resources, and providing professional training. Through these actions, the organisation seeks to support and empower students and educators through the development of collaborative learning ecosystems.

## Collaborations and Projects

The Scientotheque's main partners in Belgium are the Marguerite Yourcenar school in Laeken, the Ursulines Institute and the Victoria Sports Centre in Koekelberg, the Saint-Charles Institute in Molenbeek and the Escale School in Woluwe-Saint-Lambert. The Scientotheque was also a partner in the *Fablab Mobile Brussels*[2] project, which brought together a number of fablabs and other technology and creation initiatives in Brussels. One of the outcomes of this project was *FabULaB'Kid* which provided workshops aimed at introducing students to fablab environments as well as the specialised tools typically found therein. The Scientotheque is also involved in developing innovative teacher support systems through partnerships with a number of European projects including: the Computer Learning Community (CAI) project[3] which seeks to empower teachers by creating collaborative spaces for the co-construction and exchange of resources, the European Space Education Resource Office (ESERO) Belgium project[4] which seeks to highlight and promote STEM skills through the use of space themes and finally the European project Dexterlab,[5] a collaboration consisting of universities in France, Greece, Spain, and Belgium, which produces a catalogue of experimental science activities based on the *do-it-yourself* nature of the *Maker* community (Nikou, 2023; Norouzi et al., 2023).

---

[1] English acronym meaning Science, Technology, Engineering, Art and Mathematics.
[2] Fablabs are digital manufacturing laboratories and are used for experimenting with computer, digital, or electronic equipment, for prototyping. They are places that support creative learning through authentic situations.
[3] CAI—Computer Learning Community, see https://cai.community/.
[4] The ESERO Belgium project, funded by the European Space Agency and Belspo, offers resources and training on aerospace topics. See https://eserobelgium.be/.
[5] The DexterLab project, see http://www.thedexterlab.eu/.

## The Scientotheque Library's Educational Approach to AI

With 20 years of experience in STEAM pedagogy and, more specifically, 8 years in the development of activities related to programming and *Fablabs*, the Scientotheque has recently chosen to develop educational projects around the theme of AI for young people aged 8–18. The two main axes guiding the association's actions in the field of AI education are as follows: providing young people with the tools to develop their critical thinking and ethical reflection on its use, and supporting teachers in the discovery and transmission of digital culture and its appropriation.

The Scientotheque methodology approaches the theme of AI through the lens of the project's pedagogy. The activities are designed with a focus on experimentation, while encouraging the participation of young people in the process of creation and understanding, and collaboration. The skills and knowledge developed through this approach are considered by Papert and Harel (1991) to have better integration and transferability. Moreover, project-based learning supports a higher engagement in the activities developed in the Scientotheque.

## A Catalogue of Educational Resources on AI

In 2020, an initial review of educational resources on AI was carried out relating to both ethical and technical learning. This catalogue has made it possible to gather and structure, within a database, the resources already developed by different organisations in order to draw up a state-of-the-art in this field. The resulting catalogue, listing more than 200 educational sources and sites of interest, has been made available under a Creative Commons BY-SA licence and in a collaborative publishing format.[6]

From this catalogue, a complete set of pedagogical scenarios has been developed for teachers working with pupils aged 8–14. For example, one "unplugged" activity aims to discover the inventions that have marked the history of AI through a card game, while another identifies AI's

---

[6] See the catalogue of over 200 resources: https://lascientotheque.github.io/ressources-ia.

links to biological intelligence through experimentation. Some involve the programming of Thymio robots[7] or using the Scratch software, while others target ethical aspects encouraging debate on the consequences of AI's impact on society. These educational materials have been designed by La Scientotheque or were taken and adapted from previously identified free resources and made available online.[8] One of the advantages of these activities is their modular nature making it possible to follow the order suggested by the program or to compose a course adapted to one's specific needs by selecting all or part of the available educational activities.

## Teacher Support

Following the theories of constructivist pedagogy in the Piagetian tradition (Piaget, 1998) and andragogy (Knowles et al., 2014), adult learning is increasingly seen as self-directed, even self-determined. Nowadays, theoretical developments in the field of pedagogy increasingly emphasise the proactive role of the adult learner as exemplified by the rapidly evolving digital technologies that require a constant back-and-forth between learning skills and applying them. Fortunately, these digital technologies also give us individual access to a panoply of learning tools, which facilitates the role of individual choice in professional development.

It was found that the impact of training was less when it was not followed by support in the field. Indeed, once in class, the teacher finds himself or herself alone, faced with an activity that he or she does not feel he or she has mastered. As such, outreach activities carried out by external contributors present a specific interest not only for learners, but for teachers as well. Much like the pillars of support we put in place for our students, we need a system that facilitates the implementation of new pedagogical strategies for our professional educators. Perhaps by

---

[7] The Thymio robot is a small device with two independent wheels, sensors, and lights. It can be programmed for object detection and ground line detection.
[8] The entire service offer of the Scientotheque related to AI: https://www.lascientotheque.be/pour-les-pros/nos-ressources-steam/intelligence-artificielle/.

connecting teachers and outside non-profit organisations, we can create a network in which members can interact, collaborate, and continue to learn.

Training for teachers only has a significant and lasting impact if it is accompanied by support and opportunities for exchange within collaborative networks. The Scientotheque develops such monitoring and networking mechanisms including hotlines, resource co-creation spaces, conferences, and networking via sharing groups.

In order to enrich the traditional process of in-service training and drawing inspiration from the pedagogical developments mentioned above, the Scientotheque is developing a set of devices for the training of teachers in AI. In particular, it has created programs to support the implementation of STEAM resources in classes and organised scientific conferences on AI themes. Teachers have also been put in contact with doctoral students or scientists in the field of AI. Finally, the Scientotheque pilots inter-teacher collaboration networks on platforms such as the CAI platform and Facebook groups.

## Learning Activities for Better Understanding of AI in Education

A selection of activities was offered to two groups of young people aged 10–12 during the 2020–2021 school year during weekly extracurricular workshops at the Ursuline Institute in Koekelberg. This project, funded by the Brussels-Capital Region, aimed to reduce the school dropout rate for students living in disadvantaged neighbourhoods. Throughout the sessions, the young people were able to discover the history of machines, establish links with biological intelligence, understand the use of algorithms, observe and program Thymio robots using the Scratch platform, and discuss the consequences of AI on society. Over time, they have had the opportunity to approach different scientific disciplines through the lens of the scientific approach: formulating questions, creating and evaluating hypotheses in collaboration with others, testing those hypotheses, and providing feedback on the process. Through this process, students were required to utilise scientific and mathematical knowledge, including algorithmic logic, understanding the biology of the brain and nervous system, software programming, and robotics. They also applied the principle of reinforcement learning and ethics.

The experimental dimension of these activities allowed students to understand abstract concepts, which would otherwise be considered too complex for their age. By demystifying what AI is through "unplugged activities" or games, young people have access to tools that allow them to reflect critically on the technology. They become better equipped to understand their agency when leveraging AI tools and to acknowledge the often unseen, yet tangible, presence of the technology in their daily, digital lives. The collaborative nature of these activities also encourages students to consider alternative perspectives, be it collectively solving a problem or by participating in group games or debates (e.g. playing a labyrinth game that was used to reinforce the Q-learning model).

Finally, students were encouraged to make short group videos, in the format of interviews, testimonials, and scientific conferences, to share their learnings from the activities. This exercise allowed the participants to consolidate their knowledge, tap into their creativity, and improve their public speaking skills. Students exhibited both excitement and pride in sharing these videos with peers, teachers, and family members, which was captured in a final project video available on the Scientotheque[9] YouTube channel. An evaluation with the young people at the end of the year confirmed that they had enjoyed participating in the workshops. They unanimously expressed that they had enjoyed the activities and had learned a great deal. The students showed genuine enthusiasm for the activities on offer, whether "unplugged" or through the use of a computer or other technological device. The testimonials collected serve as a good indicator that the intended educational objective, namely to give meaning and interest to scientific and mathematical subjects in an engaging and fun way, had been achieved: "*I really liked when we played the binary language domino game*", "*I learned that we could do subjects that we don't necessarily like while playing, it was cool!*", "*I now know what an algorithm is*" or "*AI is actually maths*".

---

[9] Video excerpts from the 2020-2021 Scientotheque workshops on AI for young people, see https://www.youtube.com/watch?v=4PgT3yHWbsE.

## Perspectives

The initiatives in the creation of educational resources, workshops, and training on AI presented in this chapter were born from two main needs. The first is the growing need for AI education, especially for young audiences, as evidenced by recent reports on the subject from UNESCO (2021) or the European Commission (Tuomi, 2018). This education aims to enable young people to acquire and develop a solid understanding of AI: what it is, how it works, and how it is likely to influence their lives, while ensuring that it does not deepen existing inequalities.

The second is the need to create these resources and integrate them into educational programs. Indeed, with AI technology being a relatively new topic for Belgian schools (Collard et al., 2021), there are still few initiatives to define competency frameworks and the associated curricula for young audiences. UNESCO (2022) provides an overview of international AI initiatives, which serves to highlight the lag in adoption by French-speaking and Dutch-speaking countries compared to other regions of the world that already offer these types of educational programs.

In this context, the systems implemented by La Scientothèque turn out to be among the first concrete initiatives on the subject in Belgium. Our approach has thus been recognised at the federal level by the Ministry of Strategy and Support, with the recent support of a new project with a broader ambition: AI4InclusiveEducation.[10] This project, coordinated by the Scientotheque Library and involving a consortium of associations and universities, aims to develop educational content introducing AI, programming, data management, and robotics, in both French and Dutch, This educational content will be presented, optimised, and finally validated by partner associations and in educational networks, before being made available through open access to French- and Dutch-speaking educators.

---

[10] The AI4InclusiveEducation project aimed at the development of resources in French and Dutch in which the Scientotheque participates, see http://www.digit-all.be/.

## References

Ahn, J., Kim, J., & Sung, Y. (2022). The effect of gender stereotypes on artificial intelligence recommendations. *Journal of Business Research, 141*, 50–59.

Blanchard, M. (2021). Gender and science curriculum: A state of the art. *French Journal of Pedagogy. Educational Research, 212*, 109–143.

Chauhan, P. S., & Kshetri, N. (2022). The role of data and artificial intelligence in driving diversity, equity, and inclusion. *Computer, 55*(4), 88–93.

Collard, A. S., Hernalesteen, A., & Henry, J. (2021). Déconstruire les représentations médiatiques sur l'intelligence artificielle en jouant à "Qui est-ce?" *Proceedings TICEMED, 12*, 51.

Coslin, P. G. (2012). Social precariousness and deschooling. *Educational and Vocational Guidance* (41/3). http://journals.openedition.org/osp/3882

Fenoglio, P. (2021). At the heart of digital inequalities in education, social inequalities. *IFE Watch File* (139). http://veille-et-analyses.ens-lyon.fr/DA/detailsDossier.php?parent=accueil&dossier=139.

Kitsara, I. (2022). Artificial intelligence and the digital divide: From an innovation perspective. *Platforms and artificial intelligence: The next generation of competences* (pp. 245–265). Springer.

Knowles, M. S., Holton, E. F., III, & Swanson, R. A. (2014). *The adult learner: The definitive classic in adult education and human resource development*. Routledge.

Lucas, J.-F. (2020). *Covid-19, accelerating and amplifying digital divides*. Sciences Po "Digital, Governance and Sovereignty" Chair. https://hal.archives-ouvertes.fr/hal-03004991/document

Nikou, S. A. (2023). Student motivation and engagement in maker activities under the lens of the Activity Theory: A case study in a primary school. *Journal of Computers in Education*, 1–19. https://doi.org/10.1007/s40692-023-00258-y

Norouzi, B., Sharma, S., Kinnula, M., Iivari, N., Ukkola, M., Milara, I. S., Bulygin, G., uusitalo, J., & Iwata, M. (2023). Enabling children's genuine participation in digital design and fabrication: instructors' perspective. *International Journal of Technology and Design Education*, 1–25. https://doi.org/10.1007/s10798-023-09856-4

Papert, S., & Harel, I. (1991). Situating constructionism. *Constructionism, 36*(2), 1–11.

Piaget, J. (1998). *Of pedagogy*. Odile Jacob.

Sartori, L., & Bocca, G. (2023). Minding the gap(s): Public perceptions of AI and socio-technical imaginaries. *AI & Society, 38*(2), 443–458.

Stypinska, J. (2023). AI ageism: A critical roadmap for studying age discrimination and exclusion in digitalized societies. *AI & Society, 38*(2), 665–677.

Tuomi, I. (2018). *The impact of artificial intelligence on learning, teaching, and education.* Publications Office of the European Union.

UNESCO. (2021). *AI and education—Guide for policy makers* (56 pp.). United Nations Educational, Scientific and Cultural Organization. https://unesdoc.unesco.org/ark:/48223/pf0000380006

UNESCO. (2022). *K-12 AI curricula: A mapping of government-endorsed AI curricula.* UNESCO Publishing.

**Open Access** This chapter is licensed under the terms of the Creative Commons Attribution 4.0 International License (http://creativecommons.org/licenses/by/4.0/), which permits use, sharing, adaptation, distribution and reproduction in any medium or format, as long as you give appropriate credit to the original author(s) and the source, provide a link to the Creative Commons license and indicate if changes were made.

The images or other third party material in this chapter are included in the chapter's Creative Commons license, unless indicated otherwise in a credit line to the material. If material is not included in the chapter's Creative Commons license and your intended use is not permitted by statutory regulation or exceeds the permitted use, you will need to obtain permission directly from the copyright holder.

# 8

# Students' Perspective on the Use of Artificial Intelligence in Education

Christelle Caucheteux, Lianne-Blue Hodgkins, Victoire Batifol, Laurent Fouché, and Margarida Romero

**Abstract** While researchers and policymakers contribute crucial insights into the technical, ethical, and systemic dimensions of AI in education, the learner's perspective introduces a different viewpoint in which their representation of AI's potential influences their perspectives and hopes for improving the learning experience. In this chapter, we focus on

---

C. Caucheteux (✉) · L.-B. Hodgkins · V. Batifol · L. Fouché
Life Bloom Academy, Cagnes-sur-Mer, France
e-mail: christelle@lifebloomacademy.com

L.-B. Hodgkins
e-mail: lianne@enjoyschool.org

V. Batifol
e-mail: victoire@enjoyschool.org

L. Fouché
e-mail: laurent@enjoyschool.org

M. Romero
Université Côte d'Azur, Nice, France
e-mail: margarida.romero@univ-cotedazur.fr; margarida.romero@unice.fr

studies which analyse the perspective of middle school students at Life Bloom Academy before and after their participation in a semester of AI acculturation activities. Throughout this designated semester, students at Life Bloom Academy embarked on a comprehensive and interdisciplinary educational journey aimed at cultivating their understanding of AI. Under the guidance of their teachers, students began their journey by delving into the philosophical nuances of human intelligence. An integral component of this educational journey involved a visit to the Maison de l'Intelligence Artificielle (MIA), where students actively participated in a diverse range of multidisciplinary activities centred around both contemporary and prospective applications of AI. The study suggests that middle school students not only display a keen awareness of the societal implications linked to the utilisation of AI but also manifest a lasting enthusiasm for the technology that extends beyond the boundaries of a traditional academic setting.

**Keywords** AI education · Students' voice · AI risks · Citizenship · Agency · Early education

## Introduction

In the integration of artificial intelligence (AI) in education, it is imperative to move beyond the perspectives of researchers and policymakers and integrate the perspective of middle schoolers. Doing so promotes inclusivity, counters potential biases, and ensures that learners have a voice in the design and integration of AI in education. In this chapter, we focus on the perspective of Higher Education students on the use of AI in education before developing a study based on middle school students who have participated in a semester of activities aiming to develop their AI literacy and their capacity to develop its creative and transformative uses.

## Higher Education Students' Perspective on the Use of AI in Education

In Higher Education (HE), the study of Meade et al. (2023) identified student opinions on the use of generative artificial intelligence, particularly applications such as ChatGPT. The results revealed that over 60% of students had a basic understanding of AI tools. The study also highlighted a number of ethical and developmental concerns including standardisation, decolonisation, the reinforcement of biases, deskilling, and the potential for impeded skill development due to an over-reliance on technology. Although the issue of academic integrity was raised, several students pointed to their use of ChatGPT as a research assistant, highlighting its function in structuring ideas rather than producing content. The resulting student recommendations called for an increased focus on acculturation to AI efforts and the implementation of alternative assessment strategies that prioritise the development of critical thinking skills. Suggestions were also made to increase student–faculty dialogue around the rules of AI use in HE environments and provide regular updates regarding AI's rapidly evolving capabilities.

In a study of more than 6,300 HE students across Germany, von Garrel and Mayer (2023) observed that two-thirds were utilising generative AI tools (e.g., ChatGPT or GPT-4) with STEM disciplines showing an increased rate of adoption, possibly due to their existing affinity for technology. In all domains, save for art, art sciences, and sports, question clarification and subject-specific concept explication are the most common uses of AI in studies. In the Social Sciences, students used AI primarily for studying literature (30.3%), for translation (28.6%), and for text creation (25.4%). Alternatively, engineering students utilised AI for research (32%), translation (30.7%), and problem-solving and decision-making (30.3%).

In Idroes et al. (2023), undergraduate students in Romania identified a range of significant benefits and drawbacks of AI use in HE. Virtual assistants, with their ability to support teachers during lessons and provide prompt responses to student questions, were acknowledged as the primary benefit of AI use (42.9%) although improved time management, enhanced interactivity, lesson personalisation, and increased engagement were also mentioned. A notable portion (52.7%) of students also highlighted universal access to AI tools and inclusivity, particularly for students with special needs, as an important benefit. When specifically surveyed about AI use in the assessment process, a significant proportion of the participants (49.5%) identified continuous, timely feedback from virtual AI assistants as a major benefit. Additionally, students also highlighted the benefits of automated exam grading and the subsequent decrease in grading errors. However, students have also expressed concerns regarding the drawbacks associated with the integration of artificial intelligence (AI) in HE. The primary concern, as indicated by a significant portion (37.4%) of the Romanian undergraduates in Idroes et al. (2023), involves the impact AI could have on interpersonal connections and how that might affect the overall quality of education. Additional concerns raised encompass potential internet addiction, reduced student-teacher interactions, and the peril of information loss resulting from system malfunctions. In Canada, online students participating in the study by Seo et al. (2021) identified the benefits of personalised learner-instructor interactions, but also noted that AI had the potential to diminish interpersonal relationships by reducing the number of human-to-human interactions. In the United Arab Emirates (UAE), a study by Farhi et al. (2023) on the impact of ChatGPT usage highlighted its popularity among students as an assistant, but also reinforced the potential for its unethical use and excessive dependency.

## Middle Schoolers Perspectives on AI

In its Digital Educational Outlook, the Organisation for Economic Co-operation and Development (OECD) provides an overview of its members' efforts to integrate generative AI in educational contexts and offers recommendations for its use going forward (OECD, 2023). As such, middle school students are exposed to AI through a variety of educational initiatives. Interestingly, even when these students are not offered access to AI acculturation programmes, they continue to use AI tools outside of the school environment in a variety of educational contexts (e.g. completing homework). Within this context, a number of studies have focused on how middle school students perceive AI and its uses. For example, in Marrone et al. (2022), middle schoolers, when questioned about the relationship between AI and human creativity, voiced doubt about AI's ability to replicate the human creative process. Yet, while the same study showed that these students continued to believe that human creativity remained distinct and irreplaceable, there was an acknowledgement that future technical breakthroughs may enable AI to approximate human levels of creativity.

## The Life Bloom Academy

In this section, we outline an interdisciplinary project where teachers from the Life Bloom Academy, a middle school located in Cagnes-sur-Mer within the Alpes-Maritimes region of France, collaborated on a semester-long research intervention programme to acculturate their students to AI. A particular emphasis was placed on developing students' critical thinking, while they considered the ethical questions surrounding AI and its use in educational settings.

## Procedure

Prior to their visit to the *Maison de l'Intelligence Artificielle (MIA)*,[1] students participated in preparatory sessions in history, geography, and moral and civic education classes. During these sessions, students considered the question, 'What is intelligence?' and debated what constitutes its different forms. Equipped with these insights, students conducted visits to the MIA participating in STEAM-based activities and interactive demonstrations led by MIA staff. These activities served as prerequisites prior to students participating in immersive AI activities back at the Life Bloom Academy.

---

[1] For more information on the efforts of the Maison de l'Intelligence Artificielle (MIA), please refer to Chapter 6, International Initiatives and Regional Ecosystems for Supporting Artificial Intelligence Acculturation.

On the strength of these novel experiences, and having enriched their knowledge through mathematics, science, and technology lessons, the students took part in a second debate on the challenges of AI in history, geography, and moral and civic education. This debate focused on specific questions aimed at enabling students to activate their new learnings on AI. Each student, working alone or in pairs, answered the following questions: 'What are the positives and negatives of different AI uses in education?' and 'What advice would you give to AI developers?' Student responses were aggregated, revealing a number of AI use cases and their potential impact on daily life.

## Middle Student Perspectives on AI in Education

The following section presents five perspectives on AI, aggregated from student responses and collected by their teachers, representing one of the outcomes of the academy's interdisciplinary project. Students were asked to summarise how AI might impact their lives before considering the potential risks and ethical concerns around its widespread use. Two important reflections that arose from these student perspectives include the idea that AI's intelligence derives from a combination of pattern recognition and the processing of vast amounts of data and, as such, requires programming to function. Significantly, students also expressed their apprehensions regarding the possible threats posed by AI to their freedom, free will, and future professional opportunities.

### Students Perception of the Nature of AI

Upon completion of the acculturation activities, the students revealed two primary themes in regard to AI and its use cases. On one hand, they recognised the value in its ability to automate tasks citing examples such as automated check-outs machines in supermarkets and the autopilot function available in Tesla automobiles. On the other hand, students acknowledged the importance of human involvement in the training and programming of AI models, particularly when those models are expected to interact with humans such as in smart home devices. These examples underscored the students' awareness of AI's transformative impact on various aspects of daily life. One participant stressed that 'AI makes almost everything easier and automated these days, many things are possible. For example, more and more Tesla cars are equipped with autopilots. In addition, more and more professions are being replaced by AIs, such as cashiers in supermarkets.' Another anecdote, involving the voice-activated assistant Alexa, illustrated the idea that AI, while capable of evolving and learning independently, is still dependent on human input and guidance. 'AI could help people in their day-to-day work. It is a lot of work to program them, because yes, AI is nothing without humans. For example, Alexa who answers our questions orally and with whom we can have conversations is an AI and it is developing. I said "goodbye" to her when I was leaving and she said she didn't understand. So, I asked him to say "goodbye" to the people who said it to him. Now she'll give me sweet little expressions to say "goodbye" to me! She can develop on her own, which makes her an AI.' This dual awareness reflects a nuanced understanding among middle schoolers, recognising both the potential benefits of AI automation and the importance of human intervention in its training and development.

## Students' Concerns About Privacy and Social Control in the Era of AI

Students also raised concerns regarding the integration of AI into our lives and the impact that has on users' privacy and security. In anecdotes, students pointed to AI's ability to personalise the user experience (e.g. by tailoring recommendations and advertisements), but also acknowledged the ethical implications of widespread data collection and usage. 'AI can guide choices through our personal data. It offers us objects, services, and goods that correspond to our tastes. When we search and browse websites, an AI collects this data and resells it. This is why the advertisements we see are often personalised, but does this really respect our privacy? A lot of people are not comfortable with all their data being sold and, even if it is unlikely, this data can be hacked and used for blackmail.' Students also express their fear of AI's misuse given the potential for data breaches, hacking, and even the endangerment of lives in extreme cases such as hospital ransomware attacks. These concerns underscore the student's understanding of the risks AI poses to both personal security and individual freedom. 'There have even been hospitals hacked for ransom, putting the lives of others at risk! All this allows us to see that the data used by AI jeopardises our security and our freedom.' The students' apprehensions regarding the potential misuse of personal data by AI, highlighted by concerns over hacking incidents, particularly in critical settings like hospitals, underscores the broader viewpoint that the utilisation of data by AI poses significant risks to both personal security and individual freedom. Yet, students' concerns regarding AI's use are not only related to privacy, but also in relation to social control and democracy. Students underscored the urgent need for ethical considerations and robust safeguards in the widespread integration of AI technologies. 'As AI becomes more and more integrated into our lives, new risks associated with its use are emerging. Its use makes us think about the notions of privacy and security, that is to say the increased risks of hacking our data on the web. Especially since, if AI is used for bad purposes, the risks would be much greater. The new risks that must therefore be taken into account are the risks of the security of our data, our confidentiality and the malicious uses of AI such as for the establishment of a neo-totalitarian regime.' Another student added, 'AI is not human and it can meet needs. But it can impact our lives and our freedom. For example, navigation cookies (cookies) or recommendations follow us in our internet searches. When we go to a site, we accept cookies and the computer takes into account our taste for this site and can offer us similar ones. It reduces our freedom because we feel observed and it prevents us from making our own choices. We are offered things, so we are influenced. Soon, in our daily lives, AI will help us with repetitive and household tasks. But we should not completely depend on it.' These perspectives, while showing a good understanding of technology, also highlight the capacity of students to perceive its inherent risks and how its use might be abused or used unethically.

## Students Perception of AI in the Service of Sustainable Development

While some students' raised concerns regarding AI's use, others shared an optimistic view of AI as a potential solution to pressing global issues, particularly in the realms of ecological and sustainable development. The envisioned use cases ranged from optimising agricultural practices by anticipating diseases and managing water resources to deploying specialised robots for cleaning oceans. 'AI may seem like a solution to address ecological and sustainable development issues. It can help us create sustainable innovations, manage energy, organise depollution and recycling efforts, or resolve tense situations. Thanks to AI, it would be possible to optimise soil management and the yield of agricultural land by, for example, anticipating the appearance of diseases, optimising water use or adjusting production to demand. The robot might just look like a little chip that could scan the land to optimise for water, etc. To clean the oceans, we could make two types of robots, one that stays on the surface of the water to pick up the waste that is present there, it would have the shape of a small boat and it would be formed of a large pocket to collect waste. For the second type of robots, this one could go underwater to pick up trash. It would have the shape of a large fish and so that it would not scare marine animals, it would have a very large pocket to store waste.' The potential uses of AI for sustainable development extend to addressing climate change challenges, emphasising the role of AI in altering consumption habits, and preventing food waste through innovations like smart refrigerators. Students see AI as a transformative force that, if ethically and sustainably implemented, could contribute significantly to overcoming critical environmental and resource-related challenges globally. 'With the challenges of climate change, natural resources are dwindling and the risk of famine and food shortages is intensifying. A change in our habits is then necessary, and AI can help us in this change and in controlling our food consumption in order to preserve our resources. For example, we could create an AI that would prevent food waste with a smart refrigerator that would prevent us from wasting food. We could automate and improve the production of greenhouses thanks to AI, which would analyse the temperature and humidity. All this to say that AI can help us solve our global problems.' The students also acknowledged the critical role that AI can play in addressing the challenges posed by climate change and resource scarcity. The students emphasised the need for a shift in human habits to adapt to these challenges and AI is seen as a powerful ally in fostering this change. The proposed solutions, such as AI-managed smart refrigerators to prevent food waste and the automation of greenhouse production through AI analysis of environmental factors, highlight the technology's potential to enhance sustainability in food systems. Septiani et al. (2023) consider this type of use case as a form of agentic and transformative creativity made possible by AI.

## Students' Perception of the Potential of AI in Healthcare

Students have high expectations regarding the use of AI in the healthcare sector, particularly in the areas of care and treatment. The notion that AI could assist, or even replace, human professionals in certain medical tasks underscores the technology's capacity to enhance efficiency and precision in healthcare delivery. 'Another area where AI could be useful is in healthcare and more specifically in care and treatment. Indeed, AI could help, or even replace, professionals in their work by performing tasks or analyses in the medical field. AI could, for example, take care of delicate operations, without the intervention of personnel. One can imagine that it would be useful in the event of an accident. We could also use AI to optimise the treatment of diseases. If AI is able to detect and recognise them, it would be possible to make precise diagnoses, whether to prevent the first symptoms or to treat them at a more advanced stage, while monitoring the evolution and therefore adapting treatments. The advantage of this system would be to have a large database that would replace the limited experience of health(care) professionals.' Additionally, students shared their concerns regarding the potential risks for data privacy in healthcare. 'If a robot containing AI is hacked, it would be dangerous. For example, if a medical robot is hacked, it could cause deaths. The same problem applies for the use of AI in the army. If there are robots in a war, they will not be afraid to die and therefore they can do much more damage and death.' Moreover, students raised the potential risks of reducing human capacities. 'The other risk is the weakening of human capacities: if everything is done by AI and it no longer works, then what are we going to do, because we will no longer be able to do everyday things?' The students shared their concerns regarding the consequences of excessive dependence on technology and the dangers of developing an over-reliance on AI. In doing so, they stressed the need to maintain and nurture human competencies in the event of unforeseen challenges or failures in these systems.

## Students' Expectations of AI at the Service of Education

The students were also able to identify different use cases for AI in support of educational administrative tasks. 'The AI would be able to help teachers with administrative tasks. She will be able to do all the administrative things in relation to the director by helping him with accounting or sending emails. It would also be very useful to the teacher: for the roll call, the preparation of exercises and lessons, or the evaluation of learning.' The students also identified the potential for AI to personalise the learning experience by providing real-time scaffolding, lesson difficulty scaling, and ongoing, persistent feedback.

# Discussion

In this chapter, we have reviewed different studies on student acculturation to AI, focusing primarily on middle school and Higher Education students. We can observe that a majority of students in Higher Education use generative AI tools, such as ChatGPT, even when they have a disparate understanding of how AI works. For its part, Higher Education continues to deal with concerns around deskilling and dependency as potential impacts of AI's use. Middle schoolers are also using generative AI and reflecting on its ability to reproduce human creativity.

In order to better understand student perspectives of AI usage in educational environments, the Life Bloom Academy developed an interdisciplinary action-research activity for middle school students exploring the impact of AI on critical thinking and ethics. The project helped students comprehend AI and its ramifications, emphasising both its potential as well as ethical problems. Reflections collected from the project showed that students have high expectations in relation to AI and its different use cases. At the same time, they are also aware of the potential opportunity costs associated with AI use such as deskilling due to over-reliance and the potential for data theft and misuse. The work of the disciplinary team, based on five pedagogical inputs, allowed students to express themselves autonomously about their citizenship in the age of AI. Importantly, the experiences shared by these middle school students have shown the ability to critically analyse the potential and risks associated with AI use, but the depth and accuracy of their analysis is dependent on their understanding of AI fundamentals. Therefore, we should view acculturation to AI as a basic requirement for all students as a way of developing their citizenship and agency in the age of AI.

# References

Farhi, F., Jeljeli, R., Aburezeq, I., Dweikat, F. F., Al-shami, S. A., & Slamene, R. (2023). Analyzing the students' views, concerns, and perceived ethics about chat GPT usage. *Computers and Education: Artificial Intelligence, 5*, 100180.

Idroes, G. M., Noviandy, T. R., Maulana, A., Irvanizam, I., Jalil, Z., Lensoni, L., Lala, A., Abas, A. H., Tallei, T. E., & Idroes, R. (2023). Student perspectives on the role of artificial intelligence in education: A survey-based analysis. *Journal of Educational Management and Learning, 1*(1), 8–15.

Marrone, R., Taddeo, V., & Hill, G. (2022). Creativity and artificial intelligence - A student perspective. *Journal of Intelligence, 10*(3), 65.

Meade, M., Ogundamisi, R., & Tiratelli, M. (2023). *"Stay calm and educate" ChangeMaker-funded project investigating SRI students' perspectives on generative AI*. University College London.

OECD. (2023). Emerging governance of generative AI in education. In *OECD digital education outlook 2023: Towards an effective digital education ecosystem*. OECD iLibrary. Retrieved December 31, 2023, from https://www.oecd-ilibrary.org/sites/2a73a245-en/index.html?itemId=/content/component/2a73a245-en

Seo, K., Tang, J., Roll, I., Fels, S., & Yoon, D. (2021). The impact of artificial intelligence on learner–instructor interaction in online learning. *International Journal of Educational Technology in Higher Education, 18*(1), 1–23.

Septiani, D. P., Kostakos, P., & Romero, M. (2023, July). Analysis of creative engagement in AI tools in education based on the# PPai6 framework. In International Conference in *Methodologies and intelligent systems for technology enhanced learning* (pp. 48–58). Springer.

von Garrel, J., & Mayer, J. (2023). Artificial intelligence in studies—Use of ChatGPT and AI-based tools among students in Germany. *Humanities and Social Sciences Communications, 10*(1), 1–9.

**Open Access** This chapter is licensed under the terms of the Creative Commons Attribution 4.0 International License (http://creativecommons.org/licenses/by/4.0/), which permits use, sharing, adaptation, distribution and reproduction in any medium or format, as long as you give appropriate credit to the original author(s) and the source, provide a link to the Creative Commons license and indicate if changes were made.

The images or other third party material in this chapter are included in the chapter's Creative Commons license, unless indicated otherwise in a credit line to the material. If material is not included in the chapter's Creative Commons license and your intended use is not permitted by statutory regulation or exceeds the permitted use, you will need to obtain permission directly from the copyright holder.

# Part III

## Artificial Intelligence in Higher Education

# 9
# Affordances for AI-Enhanced Digital Game-Based Learning

Margarida Romero, Petros Lameras, and Sylvester Arnab

**Abstract** This chapter investigates the dynamic synergy between pedagogy, social dynamics, and technological developments in Digital Game-Based Learning (DGBL), which is enhanced by artificial intelligence (AI). The chapter navigates through educational modifications, learner profiling challenges, social enhancements, and technical considerations, emphasising AI's revolutionary influence. The topic expands on the critical interaction between learning analytics and machine learning, demonstrating AI's promise for personalised and adaptable DGBL experiences. The practical ramifications of real-time feedback in AI-driven DGBL are discussed, with the goal of providing timely instruction

---

M. Romero (✉)
Université Côte d'Azur, Nice, France
e-mail: margarida.romero@univ-cotedazur.fr; margarida.romero@unice.fr

P. Lameras · S. Arnab
Coventry University, Coventry, UK
e-mail: ab3430@coventry.ac.uk

S. Arnab
e-mail: aa8110@coventry.ac.uk

© The Author(s) 2024
A. Urmeneta and M. Romero (eds.), *Creative Applications of Artificial Intelligence in Education*, Palgrave Studies in Creativity and Culture,
https://doi.org/10.1007/978-3-031-55272-4_9

and encouraging positive behaviours. Finally, the chapter sheds light on the collaborative evolution of AI-enhanced education, providing useful insights for educators, instructional designers, and developers in creating optimised digital learning environments.

**Keywords** Learning analytics · Digital Game-Based Learning · Affordances · Feedback · Learner modelling

# Introduction

Playful learning environments, particularly those utilising Digital Game-Based Learning (DGBL), have reunited a diverse community of research which aims to design and evaluate the use of DGBL in different educational settings. With the advent of learning analytics and artificial intelligence (AI), these environments now offer enhanced pedagogical and social affordances. This chapter explores the intersection of these affordances, pedagogy, and AI within playful learning environments, delving into the technical, pedagogical, and social aspects that contribute to their effectiveness.

# Design Affordances for AI Tools in Education

Game design is an essential activity in game studies which aims to provide the frameworks for ensuring the alignment between the game objectives, learning mechanics (Menon & Romero, 2020; Nadolny et al., 2017; Proulx et al., 2017), game mechanics, and the playful experience of learning. In game design, affordances are not always explicitly defined. We can consider three types of affordances including pedagogical, social, and technical affordances. These three types of affordances are intricate and interdependent. Technical affordances provide the foundation, offering support for the implementation of pedagogical and social design activities. However, the effectiveness of learning is significantly influenced by the thoughtful integration of pedagogical and social affordances. Effective game design can support the synergy between these three types of affordances, facilitating a dynamic and adaptive learning environment.

## Pedagogical Affordances in AI Tools for Education

The integration of AI into DGBL introduces a transformative approach to education, offering dynamic and personalised learning experiences. AI's adaptive capability allows for real-time modifications in response to the learner/player's profile, ensuring a customised and engaging journey through the DGBL. This adaptability operates at the speed of the learner's progression, contributing to the enrichment and improvement of data accuracy for more effective, actionable, and adaptive feedback and flow balancing (Gaurav et al., 2022).

Affordances derive from the information structure of the environment and the sensory capabilities of the AI agent (virtual or physical), emerging through the interaction between the learner–player and the DGBL system integrating AI capabilities. In the context of game-based learning, AI-driven learning analytics can leverage these affordances to enhance the interactive and adaptive elements of the gaming environment. Pedagogical affordances in playful learning environments encompass various pedagogical approaches and learning activities facilitated by information and communication technology (ICT) tools.

Essentially, an affordance means the property of a system which allows certain actions to be performed, and which encourage specific types of behaviour that might determine how technology could possibly be used (Lameras et al., 2012; Kalmpourtzis & Romero, 2020). The concept of affordance may have a positive impact in terms of providing a richer understanding of the pedagogical design inherent to AI tools that would profoundly lead to an enhanced AI-based learning experience. The hallmark of AI in DGBL encompasses its adaptive capability, enabling real-time modifications aligned with the learner's profile. This adaptability operates at the learner's pace, contributing to enriched data accuracy and fostering more effective, actionable feedback. The affordance of personalisation (e.g. Lameras et al., 2021; Luckin & Cukurova, 2019) may discern customised and engaging learning journeys, tailoring content and challenges based on individual learner profiles. This affordance creates a dynamic and responsive in-game learning interaction by modifying content and challenges on-the-fly. Furthermore, this adaptability ensures that the learning journey remains challenging yet attainable, catering to the individual needs and pace of each learner (e.g. Hou et al., 2021).

Examples include problem-based learning, project-based learning, case-based learning, inquiry-based learning, and game-based learning. AI, when integrated into DGBL environments, enhances the adaptability and customisation of these pedagogical approaches, providing personalised learning experiences tailored to individual student needs (Lampropoulos, 2023).

The challenge of learner/player profiling is substantial, considering the multifaceted influences of intrinsic and extrinsic factors such as personality, motivation, interest, mood, and external events (Nacke, 2018; Tondello & Nacke, 2020). Understanding player traits becomes crucial for tailoring personalisations that influence both gameplay and learning experiences, recognising the diverse composition of individuals. Future endeavours should focus on leveraging AI to comprehensively understand players and learners through incremental and iterative profiling.

DGBLs serve as invaluable sources of data for training AI, aiming to deepen the understanding of learners and enhance personalised experiences. Current efforts predominantly centre on utilising video games to train AI algorithms, leveraging the structured progression inherent in game design. Google's DeepMind AI exemplifies this approach, building predictive models based on extensive learning from thousands of 'Go' games (Silver et al., 2017) and achieving 'Grandmaster' status in 'Starcraft II' (Vinyals et al., 2019).

AI advancements in mastering real-time strategy present opportunities for intelligently staging and scaffolding the learning experience. Rather than focusing solely on creating AI players excelling at specific games, a similar approach can be applied to develop models that progressively support and offer actionable feedback to learners throughout the gameful learning process. This feedback is not only beneficial to learners but also empowers teachers to provide personalised support, fostering continuous adaptation for improved retention and learning outcomes.

Personalised and adaptive support extends beyond player interactions, as AI-driven, non-player characters (NPCs) play a pivotal role by contributing to a game's depth and storyline. Games like 'The Elder Scrolls V: Skyrim' are at the forefront of developing NPCs that learn and evolve from interactions with players and other NPCs (Yannakakis &Togelius, 2018). This industry-driven development aligns with academic research interests, signalling a shift towards more meaningful, responsive, and adaptive interactions between learners and in-game characters in the context of gameful learning scenarios. The prospect of intelligent NPCs enhances the realism of educational game environments, fostering a more immersive and personalised learning experience.

## Social Affordances in AI for Education

AI systems can intricately develop, analyse, and leverage player/learner profiles in an incremental and iterative manner, aiming to deliver intentional experiences that consider various factors influencing motivation (Arnab, 2020). This evolving landscape in AI aligns with the exploration of social affordances, emphasising the potential for AI in education to foster tailored and socially connected learning experiences.

Social affordances focus on creating a conducive social context within ICT tools for learners' interactions. Safety, comfort, and convenience are crucial aspects. Ensuring students feel safe to express themselves involves considerations such as privacy settings and moderation. Establishing a comfortable environment requires clear ground rules, which can be supported by the presence of moderators or by a DGBL design in which the social interaction is modelled in order to be monitored and regulated by an adaptive system. Convenience is facilitated by supporting various communication modalities (text, audio, video) and synchronous/asynchronous discussions. AI can contribute by analysing emotions (Li et al., 2023) and social interactions, ensuring a positive and inclusive online atmosphere.

## Technical Affordances in AI for Education

Technical affordances pertain to the capacity and usability of ICT tools. The availability of different versions, each catering to specific needs, ensures flexibility. Usability, including interface design, ease of use, and technical support, directly influences the effectiveness of the tool. While technical affordances are necessary, they alone do not guarantee successful learning outcomes. The interplay of pedagogical and social affordances is crucial, emphasising that effective design relies on the synergy between technology and instructional and social designs.

## Affordances Perception, Learning Analytics, and Machine Learning

The recognition and utilisation of affordances in human interaction with playful learning environments constitute a pivotal aspect of adaptive digital game-based learning (DGBL). The literature review of Banihashem et al. (2023) shows the capacity of learning analytics to support dynamic and adaptive DGBL environments where learners can follow and adjust their learning based on their own specific needs.

As individuals engage with DGBL adaptive environments, they can benefit from learning analytics when they engage with the designed affordances during their play activity. This interaction sets the stage for the generation of specific learning analytics, opening avenues for diverse analytical approaches, with machine learning emerging as a particularly promising avenue.

In DGBL, machine learning based on learning analytics refers to the utilisation of machine learning algorithms to enhance the analytical process of assessing learning analytics to identify certain aspects of the learning process during DGBL interactions. The primary objective is to leverage these insightful learning analytics to inform the adaptive DGBL environment in support of learning processes. This application of machine learning holds the potential to provide additional opportunities to support the way learning analytics are analysed, offering educators and administrators a data-driven approach for adaptive DGBL.

In the context of digital game-based maths learning environments (maths DGBLE), Dai et al. (2023), used unsupervised machine learning (Gaussian Mixture Model), which permitted six clusters of 'learning-support-use' behaviours including skills development, conceptual knowledge, metacognitive connections, metacognitive regulation, information selection using cognitive aids, and sustained motivation for necessary practices. Thanks to the identification of these six clusters of 'learning-support-use' behaviours researchers proposed an adaptive system, which has improved learners' performance in the maths DGBLE environment.

In DGBL, the affordances embedded in game-based learning tools wield significant influence in learner-player interactions within the system, and as such, will also influence the type of learning analytics the system can produce. The learner's perception and utilisation of these affordances contribute to the creation of distinct learning analytics. These analytics, once generated, serve a dual purpose—they become valuable tools for the in-depth analysis of learning activities and, simultaneously, facilitate the dynamic adaptation of the DGBL system. This adaptive capability is pivotal in tailoring the educational experience to individual learner needs, enhancing the overall efficacy of digital learning environments.

The work of Hallifax et al. (2021) adds depth to this discourse through the introduction of a dynamic gamification framework. In their framework, engagement indicators play a pivotal role, functioning as the linchpin for the adaptive capabilities of the DGBL system. The proposed framework aligns with the contemporary shift towards personalised and engaging educational experiences. By leveraging engagement indicators, the system not only gauges learner involvement, but also actively adapts, ensuring sustained engagement and fostering an enriched learning process.

In the broader context of educational technology research, the exploration of affordances, learning analytics, and dynamic adaptation mechanisms represents a crucial frontier. As technology continues to shape the educational landscape, understanding how learners perceive and engage with digital tools becomes paramount. This research not only contributes to theoretical frameworks, but also holds practical implications for educators, instructional designers, and developers seeking to optimise digital learning environments for enhanced educational outcomes.

## Discussion

The integration of pedagogical, social, and technical affordances, augmented by AI capabilities, transforms playful learning environments into dynamic spaces conducive to effective and personalised learning experiences. Emphasising the importance of a balanced approach, this chapter underscores the collaborative relationship among these affordances, shedding light on the evolving landscape of AI-enhanced education.

We have highlighted the importance of learning analytics as a construct for student progress visualisation and representation into DGBL. This systematic collection, analysis, and interpretation of data generated by learners' interaction with the game environment may lead to identifying the root of any misconceptions or lack of prior knowledge that a learner may experience during game play (de Freitas et al., 2023), thereby deriving meaningful insights into individual and collective learning patterns, and areas of strength or challenges (Holstein et al., 2018). Performance metrics through dedicated AI algorithms can track progression and completion rates (Kent & Cukurova, 2020), accuracy in collaborative problem solving (Sun et al., 2020), or efficiency in learning through inquiry (e.g. Lameras & Arnab, 2021). It can be argued therefore that feedback in AI-driven DGBL, as an affordance, goes beyond traditional assessments. It is a dynamic and continuous process, providing timely and relevant information to learners and educators alike. This particular affordance may increase the quality of the feedback process by placing the focus, not only on the informative aspect of identifying potential student misunderstandings, but more importantly, by generating feedback that is actionable and contributes to a continuous improvement cycle. For example, by enabling real-time, formative feedback, learner actions may be addressed, analysed, and represented as they occur within the game. This immediacy enhances the learning experience by providing instant guidance, corrections, reflections, or reinforcement, encouraging positive behaviours, and promptly correcting misconceptions, leading to an increased understanding of the problem and how it can be resolved (Mavrikis et al., 2007; Neto & Fernandes, 2019). This aligns with the notion of personalisation, afforded by AI, as an extension to feedback mechanisms. When tailored to individual learner profiles, this feedback can target insights that guide learners towards improvements in areas requiring attention. Finally, when affordances are coupled with gamified elements such as achievements, missions, and rewards, and aligned with a playful learning environment, they may contribute to a positive and immersive learning experience, helping learners to persist in their educational journey (Conati & Kardan, 2013; Pareto, 2014).

## References

Arnab, S. (2020). *Game science in hybrid learning spaces*. Routledge. https://doi.org/10.4324/9781315295053

Banihashem, S. K., Dehghanzadeh, H., Clark, D., Noroozi, O., & Biemans, H. J. (2023). Learning analytics for online game-based learning: A systematic literature review. *Behaviour & Information Technology*, 1–28. https://doi.org/10.1080/0144929X.2023.2255301

Conati, C., & Kardan, S. (2013). Student modeling: Supporting personalized instruction, from problem solving to exploratory open ended activities. *AI Magazine, 34*(3), Article 3. https://doi.org/10.1609/aimag.v34i3.2483

Dai, C. P., Ke, F., Pan, Y., & Liu, Y. (2023). Exploring students' learning support use in digital game-based math learning: A mixed-methods approach using machine learning and multi-cases study. *Computers & Education, 194*, 104698.

de Freitas, S., Uren, V., Kiili, K., Ninaus, M., Petridis, P., Lameras, P., Dunwell, I., Arnab, S., Jarvis, S., & Star, K. (2023). Efficacy of the 4F feedback model: A game-based assessment in university education. *Information, 14*(2), Article 99. https://doi.org/10.3390/info14020099

Gaurav, D., Kaushik, Y., Supraja, S., Yadav, M., Gupta, M. P., & Chaturvedi, M. (2022). Empirical study of adaptive serious games in enhancing learning outcome. *International Journal of Serious Games, 9*(2), 27–42.

Hallifax, S., Serna, A., Marty, J. C., & Lavoué, E. (2021, April). *Dynamic gamification adaptation framework based on engagement detection through learning analytics*. Companion Proceedings of the 11th International Conference on Learning Analytics & Knowledge LAK21.

Holstein, K., McLaren, B. M., & Aleven, V. (2018, June 27–30). Student learning benefits of a mixed-reality teacher awareness tool in AI-enhanced classrooms. In *Artificial intelligence in education: 19th international conference, AIED, Proceedings, Part I 19* (pp. 154–168). Springer International Publishing.

Hou, X., Nguyen, H. A., Richey, J. E., Harpstead, E., Hammer, J., & McLaren, B. M. (2021). Assessing the effects of open models of learning and enjoyment in a digital learning game. *International Journal of Artificial Intelligence in Education*. https://doi.org/10.1007/s40593-021-00250-6

Lameras, P., & Arnab, S. (2021). Power to the teachers: An exploratory review on artificial intelligence in education. *Information, 13*(1), 14.

Lameras, P., Arnab, S., De Freitas, S., Petridis, P., & Dunwell, I. (2021). Science teachers' experiences of inquiry-based learning through a serious game: A phenomenographic perspective. *Smart Learning Environments, 8*(1), Article 7. https://doi.org/10.1186/s40561-021-00152-z

Lameras, P., Levy, P., Paraskakis, I., & Webber, S. (2012). Blended university teaching using virtual learning environments: Conceptions and approaches. *Instructional Science, 40*(1), 141–157. https://doi.org/10.1007/s11251-011-9170-9

Lampropoulos, G. (2023). Augmented reality and artificial intelligence in education: Toward immersive intelligent tutoring systems. In *Augmented reality and artificial intelligence: The fusion of advanced technologies* (pp. 137–146). Springer.

Li, Y. C., Yang, K. H., & Chang, C. H. (2023). Development and implementation of a game-based learning system with real-time facial emotion recognition technology. *IIAI Letters on Informatics and Interdisciplinary Research, 4*, 1.

Kalmpourtzis, G., & Romero, M. (2020). Constructive alignment of learning mechanics and game mechanics in Serious Game design in Higher Education. *International Journal of Serious Games, 7*(4), 75–88.

Kent, C., & Cukurova, M. (2020). Investigating collaboration as a process with theory-driven learning analytics. *Journal of Learning Analytics, 7*(1). https://doi.org/10.18608/jla.2020.71.5

Mavrikis, M., Maciocia, A., & Lee, J. (2007). *Towards predictive modelling of student affect from web-based interactions*. Proceedings of the 2007 Conference on Artificial Intelligence in Education: Building Technology Rich Learning Contexts That Work, pp. 169–176.

Menon, D., & Romero, M. (2020). Game mechanics supporting a learning and playful experience in educational escape games. In *Global perspectives on gameful and playful teaching and learning* (pp. 143–162). IGI Global.

Nadolny, L., Alaswad, Z., Culver, D., & Wang, W. (2017). Designing with game-based learning: Game mechanics from middle school to higher education. *Simulation & Gaming, 48*(6), 814–831.

Neto, A. J. M., & Fernandes, M. A. (2019). *Chatbot and conversational analysis to promote collaborative learning in distance education.* 2019 IEEE 19th International Conference on Advanced Learning Technologies (ICALT), 2161-377X, pp. 324–326. https://doi.org/10.1109/ICALT.2019.00102

Pareto, L. (2014). A teachable agent game engaging primary school children to learn arithmetic concepts and reasoning. *International Journal of Artificial Intelligence in Education, 24*(3), 251–283. https://doi.org/10.1007/s40593-014-0018-8

Proulx, J. N., Romero, M., & Arnab, S. (2017). Learning mechanics and game mechanics under the perspective of self-determination theory to foster motivation in digital game based learning. *Simulation & Gaming, 48*(1), 81–97.

Silver, D., Schrittwieser, J., Simonyan, K., Antonoglou, I., Huang, A., Guez, A., Hubert, T., Baker, L., Lai, M., Bolton, A., Chen, Y., Lillicrap, T., Hui, F., Sifre, L., van den Driessche, G., Graepel, T., & Hassabis, D. (2017). Mastering the game of go without human knowledge. *Nature, 550,* 354–359.

Sun, C., Shute, V. J., Stewart, A., Yonehiro, J., Duran, N., & D'Mello, S. (2020). Towards a generalized competency model of collaborative problem solving. *Computers & Education, 143,* 103672. https://doi.org/10.1016/j.compedu.2019.103672

Tondello, G. F., & Nacke, L. E. (2018). Gamification: Tools and techniques for motivating users. In *Extended abstracts of the 2018 CHI conference on human factors in computing systems—CHI EA 2018.* ACM. https://doi.org/10.1145/3170427.3170662

Tondello, G. F., & Nacke, L. E. (2020). Validation of user preferences and effects of personalized gamification on task performance. *Frontiers in Computer Science, 2,* 29.

Vinyals, O., Babuschkin, I., Czarnecki, W. M., et al. (2019). Grandmaster level in StarCraft II using multi-agent reinforcement learning. *Nature.* https://doi.org/10.1038/s41586-019-1724-z

Yannakakis, G. N., & Togelius, J. (2018). *Artificial intelligence and games.* Springer.

**Open Access** This chapter is licensed under the terms of the Creative Commons Attribution 4.0 International License (http://creativecommons.org/licenses/by/4.0/), which permits use, sharing, adaptation, distribution and reproduction in any medium or format, as long as you give appropriate credit to the original author(s) and the source, provide a link to the Creative Commons license and indicate if changes were made.

The images or other third party material in this chapter are included in the chapter's Creative Commons license, unless indicated otherwise in a credit line to the material. If material is not included in the chapter's Creative Commons license and your intended use is not permitted by statutory regulation or exceeds the permitted use, you will need to obtain permission directly from the copyright holder.

# 10

# Generative Artificial Intelligence in Higher Education

Margarida Romero, Jonathan Reyes, and Panos Kostakos

**Abstract** Generative Artificial Intelligence (GAI) has become popular recently with the advances in text and image generation tools (e.g., ChatGPT) that are easy to use for the general public. The emergence of GAI has sparked a surge in academic studies within higher education (HE) but also raised concerns about the changes related to policy making. This chapter analyses the impact of GAI on HE, addressing its uses in language learning, chatbot applications, and responsible AI implementation. Evaluating both its benefits and limitations, this chapter navigates through diverse studies, presenting insights into GAI's

---

M. Romero (✉) · J. Reyes
Université Côte d'Azur, Nice, France
e-mail: margarida.romero@univ-cotedazur.fr; margarida.romero@unice.fr

J. Reyes
e-mail: Jonathan.REYES-MARIMON@univ-cotedazur.fr

P. Kostakos
University of Oulu, Oulu, Finland
e-mail: panos.kostakos@oulu.fi

potential in education, while emphasising the need for responsible deployment and ethical considerations.

**Keywords** Generative Artificial Intelligence (GAI) · Higher education · ChatBots · Assessment

## Introduction

Generative Artificial Intelligence (GAI) was not a popular discussion topic among faculty in Higher Education (HE) until the emergence of tools such as ChatGPT. Since 2021, the academic discourse both in relation to policies in the use of AI, but also in relation to the potential opportunities of AI for education, has started to rise as a research topic (Southworth et al., 2023). Given the widespread availability of generative AI tools like ChatGPT, it is imperative for Higher Education Institutions (HEI) to carefully examine the practical applications and possible difficulties of AI for both professors and students. Although we must acknowledge the potential applications of AI, it is crucial to address the issue of regulating its use in the context of university work undertaken by undergraduate and graduate students. Rudolph et al. (2023) point to the challenges facing HE institutions that continue to use traditional assessment strategies when the availability of tools such as ChatGPT makes it difficult to evaluate the originality of student work. Conversely, AI can be used to scaffold student learning and create more personalised HE experiences.

GAI typically refers to advanced technology that integrates deep learning models, trained on extensive datasets, gathered from various public sources, user-generated content, licensed third-party data, and information created by human reviewers (OpenAI, 2023). This technology processes human inputs, commonly known as *prompts*, and generates outputs that closely mimic human-generated content, predominantly in the form of text and images (Lim et al., 2023). Due to their large scale, software developers building these tools utilise models that frequently lack direct insights about the quality and type of data used for training. Additionally, they are often unable to meet data retention or privacy requirements given their inability to store these data models in their independent computing environments. Hence, similar to using a search engine, a typical user currently relies on remote server interactions when exchanging data through AGI tools. This raises significant concerns regarding privacy and the potential for information leakage. This issue is particularly acute with AGI tools like ChatGPT, which require more detailed text input, in contrast to typical search engines that respond to relatively brief search queries.

In this chapter, we address these different domains by analysing the uses of AI in HE, with a special focus on generative AI. The second section addresses AI for language learning and translation in HE. The third section explores the use of conversational agents (i.e., chatbots) at the university level, while the last section addresses the responsible uses of AI in HE with a special focus on the role of assessments.

## Uses of AI in Higher Education

In their 2023 literature review, Baidoo-Anu and Ansah focused on General Artificial Intelligence (GAI) and education-related papers published in English-language, peer-reviewed journals. The review aimed to achieve two primary objectives: to evaluate the various methods of interacting with ChatGPT, and to discern the advantages and disadvantages of integrating GAI into educational practices. Within this framework, the authors introduced a typology categorising the observed benefits of employing GAI in education, encompassing areas such as personalised tutoring, Automated Steady Grading (AGS), language translation, interactive learning, and adaptive learning. Simultaneously, the review outlined a series of limitations associated with these AI applications, including the lack of human interaction, limited understanding of the technology, potential biases in training data sets, lack of creativity, dependency on the data available or generated for AI training, lack of contextual understanding, limited ability to personalise instruction, and privacy concerns. This detailed exploration of both benefits and limitations contributes to a more nuanced understanding of the impact of General Artificial Intelligence (GAI) in the realm of HE andragogy.

Several exploratory studies have applied prompt engineering (Lee et al., 2023) to more effectively examine how the GPT-3.5 model aligns with educational objectives and its suitability for such purposes. The primary methodology involves analysing the model's responses and evaluating their congruence with educational objectives. This assessment is conducted through a self-study approach as introduced by Hamilton et al. (2009). Cooper (2023) utilised ChatGPT by presenting it with a series of questions designed to elicit responses providing practical guidance for teachers on classroom applications. Findings suggest that ChatGPT performs well in generating teaching units, rubrics, and quizzes. Additionally, the results indicate that ChatGPT can aid educators in the creation of science education units structured around the 5Es model (Engage, Explore, Explain, Elaborate, Evaluate), thereby assisting in the transition from initial ideas to fully developed educational units.

Similarly, Qadir (2023) examined ChatGPT's role in engineering education, underscoring its potential as a generative AI tool across technically demanding educational settings. The research employs structured prompts as a method for eliciting detailed AI responses that facilitate various real-life educational applications. Although not based on a specific pedagogical framework, the study provides empirical evidence of ChatGPT's utility in engineering education. Its applications span technical subjects like coding and mathematics, creative writing, virtual tutoring, personalised learning, test preparation, and language learning. Conversely, some of the disadvantages include the lack of human interaction in providing personalised feedback to learners. Moreover, as the study involved an older model of ChatGPT (i.e., GPT-3.5 architecture), concerns regarding reliability, plagiarism, and hallucinative misinformation were noted as potential shortcomings when using automated feedback. The paper also emphasises the growing importance of prior knowledge and critical thinking, given their importance in creating prompts that generate quality responses.

Chan (2023) has studied the use of text-generative AI technologies in Hong Kong universities to develop a framework for the integration of AI into education. The study engaged 457 students and 180 faculty and staff members. Chan has identified three dimensions: the pedagogical dimension, the governance dimension, and the operational dimension in the integration of AI in higher education. Within the context of HE andragogy, Chan's framework (2023) highlights the importance of reengineering the assessment process given the innovative methodologies made possible through the use of AI. In this sense, both the automatic analysis, as well as the exploitation of learning analytics for assessment purposes (Ouyang et al., 2023) were examined. Similarly, the pedagogical dimension is also where Chan stresses the importance of developing the transversal competencies considered critical for future success in the innovation economy (Septiani et al., 2023).

Within the *governance dimension*, senior leadership plays a pivotal role in addressing the complex considerations related to AI implementation in education. This encompasses strategies to understand, identify, and prevent academic misconduct and ethical dilemmas facilitated by AI, as well as the establishment of robust policies and protocols for data privacy, transparency, accountability, and security in AI usage. In this sense, the AI Act, developed at the European level, aims to develop trustworthy AI (Laux et al., 2023). The AI Act postulates different requirements for 'trustworthy' AI: human agency and oversight, technical robustness and safety, privacy and data governance, transparency, diversity, accountability, non-discrimination and fairness, societal and environmental well-being, and accountability (EC, 2019). Furthermore, the *governance dimension* extends to AI attribution and the clear definition of roles and responsibilities for the technology's implementation and management, thereby ensuring accountability for its ethical use within the institution. Equally significant is the commitment to ensuring equity in access to AI technologies, achieved through implementing measures that guarantee fair and inclusive access to AI resources for all students and faculty, while also addressing potential disparities in AI utilisation across different demographic groups.

The *operational dimension*, involving teaching and learning stakeholders as well as IT staff, centres on the practical aspects of AI implementation in university settings. This includes establishing robust monitoring mechanisms to assess the effectiveness of AI integration and continuously evaluating its impact on teaching, learning, and overall educational outcomes. Moreover, this dimension encompasses comprehensive training programmes and ongoing support structures that enhance AI literacy among faculty, staff, and students, while addressing the challenges and benefits of proficient AI use across the university.

Sabzalieva and Valentini's (2023) guide on the use of generative AI in HE develops an introduction to the technology and provides different use cases as an interactive tool fulfilling the role of tutor, socratic opponent, or even co-designer.

## AI for Language Learning and Translation

The prevalent use of English in research studies, publications, and competitive grants at the international level creates an inclusivity barrier, not only for faculty and students, but also for administrative staff who lack the necessary proficiency in English to fully participate in the academic process (Ingvarsdóttir & Arnbjörnsdóttir, 2013). This linguistic dominance reduces the opportunities and competitiveness of non-native English speakers and limits access to learning resources for students who lack English fluency. As such, AI translation tools, such as Grammarly or Quilbot, can play a pivotal role in facilitating accessibility, but also improving the overall quality of written work, from both a grammatical and contextual perspective. Implementing AI-driven translation tools can reduce language barriers such as in the case of the MSc Smart EdTech programme at the Université Côte d'Azur, where most of the students and faculty are using English as a second language. With an international cohort representing eighteen different countries, the use of real-time translation tools during synchronous, online activities helped create a more inclusive learning environment for non-fluent, English speakers. Similarly, the use of automatic note taking tools has facilitated the creation of meeting minutes and made documenting projects easier in the context of research initiatives such as the Horizon AugMentor project.

## Chatbots in Higher Education

Expanding from the pioneering work of Eliza (Weizenbaum, 1966), acknowledged as the first chatbot in academic research, the exploration of chatbot-assisted learning environments has progressed significantly over the last few decades. Nevertheless, it is in recent years that chatbots have experienced a substantial surge in both usage scenarios and research within the educational realm, reaching a pinnacle in 2023 (Hwang & Chang, 2021). The most common application of chatbots in educational settings is as a tool used to interact with predefined content learning paths, often referred to as guided learning (Akcora et al., 2018). The current availability of generative AI chatbot services and chatbot application programming interfaces (API) enables educators to add a new layer of chatbot capabilities that can support active learning approaches in education (Lo, 2023). Chatbots were created to enable natural language interaction between humans and computers. As such, chatbots can be considered as computer programmes that aim to mimic some aspects of human interaction supported by machine conversation systems, virtual agents, dialogue systems, and personal assistants all with the goal of supporting the end-user (Suhaili et al., 2021). The systematic literature review by Okonkwo and Ade-Ibijola (2021) outlines the diverse applications of chatbots in HE, including teaching and learning (66%), research and development (19%), assessment (6%), administration (5%), and advisory (4%).

Integrating chatbots into HE settings enables universities to address the specific uses outlined in the UNESCO table on the use of generative AI (see Table 10.1). This is possible due to the versatile nature of these tools and the adaptive experience they offer to users. Furthermore, the ability of chatbots to understand and generate human-like responses, known as Natural Language Processing (NLP), creates a more intuitive way for students and educators to interact with the tools (Maher et al., 2020; Rath et al., 2023), while also facilitating the personalisation of the learning experience based on individual student needs (Younis et al., 2023).

The inclusion of NLP capabilities in the training of chatbots has benefited developers and pedagogical staff seeking to personalise their use for

Table 10.1 Use of generative AI in higher education according to UNESCO

| Role | Description | Example of implementation |
|---|---|---|
| Possibility engine | AI generates alternative ways of expressing an idea | Students write queries in ChatGPT and use the Regenerate response function to examine alternative responses |
| Socratic opponent | AI acts as an opponent or can help develop an argument | Students enter prompts into ChatGPT following the structure of a conversation or debate. Teachers can ask students to use ChatGPT to prepare for discussions |
| Collaboration coach | AI helps groups research and solve problems together | Working in groups, students use ChatGPT to develop their ideas, identify resources, and complete assignments |
| Guide on the side | AI acts as a guide to navigate physical and conceptual spaces | Teachers use ChatGPT to generate content for classes/courses (e.g., discussion questions) and advice on how to support students in learning specific concepts |
| Personal tutor | AI tutors each student and provides immediate and actionable feedback on their progress | ChatGPT provides personalised feedback to students based on learning analytics provided by students or teachers (e.g., test scores) |
| Co-designer | AI assists in the learning design process | Teachers ask ChatGPT for ideas on designing or updating a curriculum (e.g., rubrics for assessment) and/or accomplishing specific learning goals (e.g., how to make the curriculum more accessible) |
| Exploratorium | AI provides tools to research, explore, and interpret data | Teachers provide basic information to students who use ChatGPT to explore the topic in more detail. ChatGPT can also be used to support language learning |

(continued)

Table 10.1 (continued)

| Role | Description | Example of implementation |
|---|---|---|
| Study buddy | AI helps the student reflect on the learning material | Students explain their current level of understanding to ChatGPT and ask for ways to help them study the material. ChatGPT could also be used to help students prepare for other tasks (e.g., job interviews) |
| Motivator | AI offers games and challenges to extend learning | Teachers or students ask ChatGPT for ideas on how to extend students' learning after providing a summary of the current level of knowledge (e.g., quizzes, exercises) |
| Dynamic assessor | AI provides educators with a profile of each student's current knowledge on a particular topic | Students interact with ChatGPT in a tutorial-type dialogue in order to produce a summary of their current state of knowledge. This is then shared with their teacher/assessor |

HE environments. Additional refinements to the personalisation process occur during tokenisation,[1] where text is converted into smaller units in order to make the chatbots more efficient and effective (Bhartiya et al., 2019). Once trained and generating responses with a high level of reliability, developers continue to monitor the chatbot's performance and provide iterative training to ensure that it is functioning smoothly and providing accurate information. Moreover, Tsivitanidou and Ioannou (2021) considers the potential of chatbots to support certain types of learning scenarios in HE.

In their guidelines, Chocarro et al. (2023) explain the desirability of empowering teaching and administrative staff to effectively use AI, even as its use continues to face questions regarding user digital literacy, ethics, data privacy, and how these tools impact current pedagogical strategies.

---

[1] Tokenisation is the process of transforming a sequence of characters into a collection of distinct tokens. In the realm of computer science, tokens encompass a variety of elements, including words, integers, identifiers, special characters, and punctuation marks (Bhartiya et al., 2019).

It is essential that a comprehensive artificial intelligence training program for university students and staff includes learning skills related to using, developing, and implementing chatbots. This inclusion is crucial at various levels:

- **Problem Identification**: Universities should support the pedagogical empowerment and the AI acculturation of operational staff to identify opportunities and problems that can be facilitated using chatbots.
- **Theoretical/Practical Framework**: Universities should provide assistance in the creation and development of chatbot-based assisted learning scenarios based on the needs of educators and learners.
- **Ubiquitousness**: Universities should ensure that the use of chatbots is democratised, widespread, and reflective of the latest technological and training iterations.
- **Practical use**: Universities should assist students in learning the skills necessary to seamlessly integrate chatbots into their learning environment.
- **Assessment**: Universities should continuously assess and refine their chatbot training models following a holistic set of quality standards.

When contemplating the implications associated with the development and application of chatbots in educational settings, educators have the responsibility to consider the role biases play in their usage and development. For instance, tokenisation, a key aspect in data processing, requires careful attention to mitigate instances of information biases and to ensure that the chatbots maintain a pedagogical perspective. Ensuring that the tokenisation of data is executed without bias is imperative, as it directly impacts the effectiveness, accuracy, fairness, and equity of the educational experience as facilitated by the chatbot (Akter et al., 2021). Furthermore, educators must advocate for the availability of chatbot APIs capable of seamlessly functioning in different languages, thereby fostering inclusivity and accommodating linguistic diversity (Mogavi et al., 2023).

Finally, the shift in AI chatbots development APIs to no-code and low-code, especially OpenAI's GPTs in November 2022 (Lim et al., 2023), marks a significant milestone in democratising chatbot development for education. This shift has a notable impact on the development and use of chatbots as it allows individuals to create their own customised AI tools without having extensive knowledge of software development or programming. In the context of educational use cases, this removes many of the significant barriers preventing educators from leveraging their unique expertise and training in the creation of their own AI tools.

## Responsible Use of Generative AI Tools in Academia

In November 2022, OpenAI made ChatGPT publicly available for free, employing the highly advanced GPT-3 model as its backbone Large Language model (LLM). By January 2023, OpenAI announced that ChatGPT had accumulated over 100 million users, setting a new global record as the fastest-growing application to date (Lim et al., 2023). The exponential growth of ChatGPT had a significant impact on the education sector, as students and educators around the world began exploring the app's novel functionalities. Delivered through an intuitive and user-friendly chatbot interface, ChatGPT's text translation, question-answering (Q&A), and text generation capabilities introduced new opportunities and challenges to modern learning and teaching values, norms, and methodologies. This development has been met with mixed reactions from the educational community, prompting educational institutions worldwide to establish ad hoc committees of experts tasked with revising their ethical frameworks, guidelines, and recommendations concerning the use of Generative AI (GAI) in education and pedagogy.

Russell Group universities provide a comprehensive framework dedicated to promoting the ethical and responsible utilisation of GAI tools within academic settings. These institutions are steadfast in their commitment to following established guidelines for the ethical use of AI tools in education, as outlined by the principles set forth by the Russell Group. This commitment involves fostering AI literacy among both students and staff and empowering educators as they guide students in the effective and responsible use of generative AI tools. Additionally, the Russell Group universities actively engage in reviewing and adapting curriculum, teaching methods, and assessment practices to seamlessly integrate the ethical use of generative AI and ensure equitable access for all. This commitment extends to upholding academic rigour and integrity, while also fostering collaboration with other institutions to share best practices in response to the evolving technological landscape and its educational applications.

## References

Akcora, D. E., Belli, A., Berardi, M., Casola, S., Di Blas, N., Falletta, S., Faraotti, A., Lodi, L., Diaz, D. N., Paolini, P., Renzi, F., & Vannella, F. (2018, June 27–30). Conversational support for education. In *Artificial intelligence in education: 19th International Conference*. AIED 2018, London, UK, 2018, Proceedings, Part II 19 (pp. 14–19). Springer.

Akter, S., McCarthy, G., Sajib, S., Michael, K., Dwivedi, Y. K., D'Ambra, J., & Shen, K. N. (2021). Algorithmic bias in data-driven innovation in the age of AI. *International Journal of Information Management, 60*, 102387.

Baidoo-Anu, D., & Ansah, L. O. (2023). Education in the era of generative artificial intelligence (AI): Understanding the potential benefits of ChatGPT in promoting teaching and learning. *Journal of AI, 7*(1), 52–62.

Bhartiya, N., Jangid, N., Jannu, S., Shukla, P., & Chapaneri, R. (2019, July). Artificial neural network based university chatbot system. In *2019 IEEE Bombay Section Signature Conference* (IBSSC) (pp. 1–6). IEEE.

Chan, C. K. Y. (2023). A comprehensive AI policy education framework for university teaching and learning. *International Journal of Educational Technology in Higher Education, 20*(1), 38.

Chocarro, R., Cortiñas, M., & Marcos-Matás, G. (2023). Teachers' attitudes towards chatbots in education: A technology acceptance model approach considering the effect of social language, bot proactiveness, and users' characteristics. *Educational Studies, 49*(2), 295–313.

Cooper, G. (2023). Examining science education in ChatGPT: An exploratory study of generative artificial intelligence. *Journal of Science Education and Technology, 32*(3), 444–452.

European Commission. (2019). *Ethics guidelines for trustworthy AI*. https://digital-strategy.ec.europa.eu/en/library/ethics-guidelines-trustworthy-ai

Hamilton, M. L., Smith, L., & Worthington, K. (2009). Fitting the methodology with the research: An exploration of narrative, self-study and autoethnography. *Studying Teacher Education, 4*(1), 17–28. https://doi.org/10.1080/17425960801976321

Hwang, G.-J., & Chang, C.-Y. (2021). A review of opportunities and challenges of chatbots in education. *Interactive Learning Environments.* https://doi.org/10.1080/10494820.2021.1952615

Ingvarsdóttir, H., & Arnbjörnsdóttir, B. (2013). ELF and academic writing: A perspective from the expanding circle. *Journal of English as a Lingua Franca, 2*(1), 123–145.

Laux, J., Wachter, S., & Mittelstadt, B. (2023). Trustworthy artificial intelligence and the European Union AI act: On the conflation of trustworthiness and acceptability of risk. *Regulation & Governance, 18*, 3–32.

Lee, U., Jung, H., Jeon, Y., Sohn, Y., Hwang, W., Moon, J., & Kim, H. (2023). Few-shot is enough: Exploring ChatGPT prompt engineering method for automatic question generation in English education. *Education and Information Technologies*, 1–33. https://doi.org/10.1007/s10639-023-12249-8

Lim, W. M., Gunasekara, A., Pallant, J. L., Pallant, J. I., & Pechenkina, E. (2023). Generative AI and the future of education: Ragnarök or reformation? A paradoxical perspective from management educators. *The International Journal of Management Education, 21*(2), 100790.

Lo, C. K. (2023). What is the impact of ChatGPT on education? A rapid review of the literature. *Education Sciences, 13*(4), 410. MDPI AG. https://doi.org/10.3390/educsci13040410

Maher, S., Kayte, S., & Nimbhore, S. (2020). Chatbots & its techniques using AI: A review. *International Journal for Research in Applied Science and Engineering Technology, 8*(12), 503–508.

Mogavi, R. H., Deng, C., Kim, J. J., Zhou, P., Kwon, Y. D., Metwally, A. H. S., Tlili, A., Bassanelli, S., Bucchiarone, A., Gujar, S., Nacke, L. E., & Hui, P. (2023). ChatGPT in education: A blessing or a curse? A qualitative study exploring early adopters' utilization and perceptions. *Computers in Human Behavior: Artificial Humans*, 100027. ISSN 2949-8821. https://doi.org/10.1016/j.chbah.2023.100027

Okonkwo, C. W., & Ade-Ibijola, A. (2021). Chatbots applications in education: A systematic review. *Computers and Education: Artificial Intelligence, 2*, 100033.

OpenAI. (2023). *Enterprise privacy*. OpenAI. Retrieved November 22, 2023 from https://openai.com/enterprise-privacy

Ouyang, F., Wu, M., Zheng, L., Zhang, L., & Jiao, P. (2023). Integration of artificial intelligence performance prediction and learning analytics to improve student learning in online engineering course. *International Journal of Educational Technology in Higher Education, 20*(1), 1–23.

Qadir, J. (2023). Engineering education in the era of ChatGPT: Promise and pitfalls of generative AI for education. In *2023 IEEE global Engineering Education Conference (EDUCON)* (pp. 1–9). IEEE.

Rath, S., Pattanayak, A., Tripathy, S., Priyadarshini, S. B. B., Tripathy, A., & Tanvi, S. (2023). Prediction of a novel Rule-Based Chatbot Approach (RCA) using natural language processing techniques. *International Journal of Intelligent Systems and Applications in Engineering, 11*(3), 318–325.

Rudolph, J., Tan, S., & Tan, S. (2023). ChatGPT: Bullshit spewer or the end of traditional assessments in higher education? *Journal of Applied Learning and Teaching, 6*(1).

Sabzalieva, E., & Valentini, A. (2023). *ChatGPT and artificial intelligence in higher education: Quick start guide*. UNESCO.

Septiani, D. P., Kostakos, P., & Romero, M. (2023, July). Analysis of creative engagement in AI tools in education based on the# PPai6 framework. In *International conference in methodologies and intelligent systems for technology enhanced learning* (pp. 48–58). Springer.

Southworth, J., Migliaccio, K., Glover, J., Reed, D., McCarty, C., Brendemuhl, J., & Thomas, A. (2023). Developing a model for AI across the curriculum: Transforming the higher education landscape via innovation in AI literacy. *Computers and Education: Artificial Intelligence, 4*, 100127.

Suhaili, S. M., Salim, N., & Jambli, M. N. (2021). Service chatbots: A systematic review. *Expert Systems with Applications, 184*, 115461.

Tsivitanidou, O., & Ioannou, A. (2021, July). Envisioned pedagogical uses of chatbots in higher education and perceived benefits and challenges. In *International conference on human-computer interaction* (pp. 230–250). Springer.

Weizenbaum, J. (1966). ELIZA—A computer program for the study of natural language communication between man and machine. *Communications of the ACM, 9*(1), 36–45.

Younis, H. A., Ruhaiyem, N. I. R., Ghaban, W., Gazem, N. A., & Nasser, M. (2023). A systematic literature review on the applications of robots and natural language processing in education. *Electronics, 12*(13), 2864.

**Open Access** This chapter is licensed under the terms of the Creative Commons Attribution 4.0 International License (http://creativecommons.org/licenses/by/4.0/), which permits use, sharing, adaptation, distribution and reproduction in any medium or format, as long as you give appropriate credit to the original author(s) and the source, provide a link to the Creative Commons license and indicate if changes were made.

The images or other third party material in this chapter are included in the chapter's Creative Commons license, unless indicated otherwise in a credit line to the material. If material is not included in the chapter's Creative Commons license and your intended use is not permitted by statutory regulation or exceeds the permitted use, you will need to obtain permission directly from the copyright holder.

# 11

# Artificial Intelligence in Professional and Vocational Training

Solange Ciavaldini-Cartaut, Jean-François Métral, Paul Olry, Dominique Guidoni-Stoltz, and Charles-Antoine Gagneur

**Abstract** This chapter explores challenges linked to AI integration in professional training, emphasising the need to question the learning analytics generated during activities involving humans or living entities. The intersection of initial and ongoing training poses a design challenge: making AI tools acceptable for both training and the workplace. This chapter critically examines the nature and quality of the initial data and learning analytics using educational data mining through three case studies of adaptive learning environments. The first case study addresses

---

S. Ciavaldini-Cartaut (✉)
Université Côte d'Azur, Nice, France
e-mail: Solange.CARTAUT@univ-cotedazur.fr

J.-F. Métral · P. Olry · D. Guidoni-Stoltz · C.-A. Gagneur
Institut Agro Dijon, Dijon, France
e-mail: jean-francois.metral@agrosupdijon.fr

P. Olry
e-mail: paul.olry@agrosupdijon.fr

D. Guidoni-Stoltz
e-mail: dominique.guidoni-stoltz@agrosupdijon.fr

the challenges of modelling Comté cheese manufacturing. The second case study describes Silva Numerica, a digital forest simulator, exploring how AI, as a learning tool, can contribute to realistic modelling while addressing didactic obstacles. The third case delves into AI's role in automotive mechanics training, emphasising the need for visibility in cognitive inference processes. The chapter concludes by addressing data reliability concerns in AI systems and proposing education and training strategies to overcome such challenges.

**Keywords** Professional training · Vocational training · Learning analytics · Artificial intelligence · Digital learning environment

# Introduction

In order to develop an AI system, it is essential to possess dependable data that can be utilised to facilitate the process of teaching and learning. In vocational training, this type of data is distinguished by its emphasis on practical knowledge and the use of informal, deliberative, and adaptable regulations in the workplace, with a focus on productivity. A second challenge in developing an AI in professional training lies in maintaining the educational value of real-life experiences, which encompass a wide range of situations, various approaches, and different outcomes. This must be done while simultaneously taking into account the applicability of real-world work scenarios for educational objectives (Ciavaldini-Cartaut et al., 2022).

The challenges of using AI-powered smart tutors present several obstacles: (i) providing feedback for human interactions over extended periods, and (ii) the absence of detailed descriptions regarding the actual work. This chapter delves into the criticisms and questions surrounding AI in professional training, specifically in the context of alternating between formal education and workplace training. The analyses are grounded in the cultural, anthropocentric, and socio-technical paradigm of technology use (Albero, 2019). AI can be considered as instruments for operations, processes, and access to information supporting the teaching-learning process (Folcher & Rabardel, 2004). While AI can enhance cooperation and support learning analytics, challenges arise in applying it to complex, 'with and for the living' activities where observable behaviours fall short in capturing the intricate cognitive, adaptive, and creative processes required in work situations. Learning analytics, in this context, proves limited in comprehending these nuanced processes (Albero, 2019).

This chapter critically examines the nature and quality of the initial data and learning analytics using educational data mining. Empirical illustrations include the adaptive reasoning challenges in Comté cheese manufacturing (Chrétien et al., 2020) and the e-Fran research, Silva Numerica (https://silvanumerica.net/), focusing on a forest management learning environment (Chiron, 2018; Guidoni-Stoltz, 2019, 2020). The latter explores how AI, as a learning tool, can contribute to realistic modelling while addressing didactic obstacles. The third illustration delves into AI's role in automotive mechanics training (Gagneur & Vassout, 2019), emphasising the need for visibility in cognitive inference processes.

## The Use of Professional Analytics in Designing AI Tools

In both social and educational contexts, discussions on professional skills and tasks abound. Yet, complexities arise when considering the actual work done within companies, primarily due to the proprietary nature of productive work and the inherent difficulties of documenting intricate work processes. Furthermore, very little is known about the specific and often diverse processes required to complete a job, particularly when that job requires collaborating with other humans in a dynamic environment.

This chapter addresses the challenge of identifying relevant data points for evaluating learning in professional environments when the work done includes a mix of discretionary and prescribed tasks. Companies often rely on procedures, but the associated knowledge is frequently disconnected from the actual complexities of real workplace activities. Furthermore, while simulations can provide more realistic situations from which to study, their effectiveness in regard to teaching or learning is well-documented within the field of professional didactics.

In the realm of school education, obtaining tangible data seems more straightforward, with established scientific and didactic knowledge. However, the world of work presents challenges where efficiency is correlated with immediate or long-term results, making judgments about individuals' work and the data associated with that work, 'awkward to say' (Dujarier, 2010). Vocational training stands at the crossroads of using tangible learning analytics (Knight & Buckingham, 2017) and data faithful to work situations (Chiron, 2018). The chapter concludes by addressing the challenges of developing AI tools or implementing machine learning algorithms for work situations, where the initial data may lack the precision necessary to foster effective learning.

## Exploring AI in Vocational Training: The Case of French Comté Cheese

The production of French Comté cheese (Chrétien et al., 2020) is well-documented and offers insights into the challenges and potential of AI in vocational training. Despite extensive data on standardised procedures, including factors like cow types, weather, and soil conditions, a crucial anthropocentric perspective reveals a gap in understanding essential variables. These variables, which influence a cheesemaker's decision-making for distinct flavours, remain elusive. As such, while procedural data could be used to train AI tools for this type of vocational environment, the inclination towards industrialised processes over contextual reasoning presents a socio-technical problem: manufacturers and management tend to prioritise procedures, not reasoning, when designing their professional training. This bias raises questions regarding data selection and the role of humans in AI design, distinct from the context of school education.

The case of Comté cheese production highlights workplace learning, prompting inquiry into how AI could impact learning in professional settings. Littlejohn (2017) notes challenges in modelling complex, dynamic environments due to inadequate information sensors. In Comté cheese manufacturing, perceptual and gestural dimensions, crucial for the cheesemaker's decision-making, lack suitable sensors for AI interpretation. The political and technical intricacies of collecting tangible analytics pose questions about industry willingness, standards, and components necessary for documenting an AI system. While high-risk industries have addressed these challenges, AI's impact in vocational training extends to other sectors, necessitating a broader exploration of its potential influence.

## AI Support in Simulated Environments: The Silva Numerica Project

One potential application of AI in vocational training is its role as a learning partner. This involves utilising AI as a support tool to enhance various aspects of professional learning. For instance, AI could help document reliable data for designing simulations that replicate work situations, especially those challenging for future professionals to access. It could also contribute to improving the handling of critical situations, be it in product development, manufacturing processes, or collaborating with people. Consider the risk-laden scenarios of taking-off and landing a commercial aircraft at a congested airport during peak travel season. An AI tool could document the processes necessary for a pilot to complete these tasks, however, it would be unable to articulate the subtle or invisible learnings, acquired through repetition, over extended periods of time. AI would face a similar challenge in documenting the processes and actions related to managing a forest within a complex ecosystem that evolves over long periods of time, absent human intervention. The Silva Numerica project (Guidoni-Stoltz, 2019, 2020) has meticulously gathered data documenting forest management work with the goal of designing a digital learning environment that can capture the intricacies of this field. Despite their efforts, the virtual simulator they developed for educational purposes encounters significant limitations. First, the natural developmental processes it seeks to replicate are inherently complex, lacking a ready-made global model for training or a comprehensive database. This complexity is further compounded by its dependence on contextual factors such as climate, commercial outlets, and specific silviculture goals and practices (Mayen & Lainé, 2014). Similar challenges are highlighted in the study by Chrétien et al. (2020) concerning cheese making. While the manufacturing process, well-documented with precise and reliable data, lends itself to potential AI development, the ways in which these processes are implemented remain implicit. Therefore, the lack of thorough data becomes apparent when considering the variability and diversity of real-world work situations. For these same reasons, the design and use of AI-powered simulators also become a challenge. Some studies, including recent work by didacticians like Vadcard (2013, 2019), underscore the nuanced nature of simulation effectiveness. They argue that achieving realism in simulating complex and dynamic environments doesn't guarantee training effectiveness. In fact, excessive realism might be counterproductive, as modifying reality for pedagogical purposes is often a prerequisite for transforming situations into meaningful learning experiences. For example, Silva Numerica's forest simulation, while relatively realistic based on regular high forest silviculture of sessile oaks, introduces a simplified representation of trees as 'lollipop sticks'. This departure from realism serves as a semiotic resource for learning, aiding in tasks like selecting trees based on their ability to contribute to forestry development.

This raises the question: to what extent can AI contribute to modelling a training process based on databases of work tasks, outside of practice situations? Furthermore, how can AI facilitate modelling and simulations when dealing with poorly documented phenomena and processes?

## The Challenges of Utilising AI and Intelligent Tutors in Professional Learning

A pivotal inquiry in our exploration pertains to the capacity of AI to furnish pertinent feedback for learning. As elucidated by Hwang et al. (2020), the concept of AI as an intelligent tutor is prevalent in the literature. The crux of AI's use in professional training resides in its ability to scrutinise learner activity and generate meaningful feedback. This poses a formidable challenge, as it hinges on the expectation that AI technologies can dissect a learner's actions on the machine, explicate the validity or invalidity of their achievements, and assess the associated learning quality. In professional domains like forest management, where diverse and context-dependent outcomes may be valid, the interpretative challenge for AI intensifies.

AI's interpretation must acknowledge that conformity with a result doesn't necessarily imply the learner's comprehension of underlying strategies, procedures, or professional knowledge. Moreover, AI's feedback cannot be solely aligned with good practice or standard reasoning, as various other legitimate reasonings may lead to comparable outcomes. Hence, establishing indicators that can evaluate a learner's acquired knowledge or identify difficulties associated with the learning experience continues to complicate the use of AI tools in these environments.

The ensuing question revolves around the potential of AI, coupled with learning analytics, to tailor guidance based on user knowledge and learning. Can AI leverage its touted abilities in machine and deep learning to detect errors or recurring difficulties, subsequently adapting its feedback to that of a human teacher? We perceive significant risks in relying solely on AI for this purpose. The self-learning capacity of artificial neural networks is constrained by their indexing to an incomplete digital image rather than reality. Additionally, AI's pursuit of concordances between datasets to extract regularities diverges from the maieutics of discrepancies inherent in tutoring practices. As suggested by Savoyant (2006), AI could be useful for a first step: to work out a task (what I have to do), but not to assimilate it (how I have to do it).

While it is conceivable that AI may achieve a level of finesse in detecting pedagogically relevant discrepancies within texts or simulated activities, challenges persist in indexing AI to remote contextual elements. In vocational training, the indexing process involves tacit professional knowledge, which may be distant from the immediate conditions of action, posing challenges in acquisition, selection, and relevance that current digitisation capabilities cannot fully automate.

The example of the Silva Numerica project underscores these challenges. Despite efforts to record learner actions and responses, the complexity of the resulting data made it challenging for trainers to conduct effective debriefings. Analytics tied to individual actions proved difficult to interpret and utilise during training, prompting a shift to follow learner activity in the virtual environment and incorporate activity data in the post-training evaluation. This pragmatic adjustment highlights the limitations of realising the idealised concept of an intelligent tutor. The integration of AI in professional learning, while holding promise, necessitates cautious consideration of the complex, nuanced nature of real-world professional situations (Casilli, 2019). Sole reliance on AI, devoid of teacher supervision, for learning maieutics and guidance based on discrepancies, remains a formidable challenge. The examples presented underscore the intricate interplay between AI and the multifaceted realities of professional training contexts.

## Conclusion: Navigating the Terrain of AI in the Field of Professional Learning

In this chapter, we began our exploration by examining the potential benefits and existing constraints surrounding the integration of AI in the instruction and acquisition of vocational skills within training programmes and workplace contexts (Ciavaldini-Cartaut et al., 2022). We elucidated a pivotal element crucial to unlocking the value of AI in these applications: the imperative of rendering work data, encompassing gestures, situations, circumstances, reasoning, and the learning data itself, both reliable and tangible.

While the trajectory of AI's evolution remains challenging to forecast due to the rapid advancements in machine learning techniques, we contend that a persistent challenge lies in tethering these processes to reality. This challenges the very essence of AI integration, extending beyond a mere technical hurdle to a fundamental, enduring constraint. Consequently, the quest for tangibility and usability of work data mandates a collaborative approach with professional organisations. This involves designing learning support tools that leverage access to such data through collaborative research initiatives, surmounting the sociotechnical barrier of professional scepticism towards work data, and facilitating access to AI-embedded work reasoning and knowledge for educators, trainers, and learners.

The realisation of tangible work data necessitates a multifaceted strategy, including the unveiling of real work nuances, the discernment of reasoning processes, and the empowerment of individuals to master AI as a tool, as articulated by Folcher and Rabardel (2004). We have underscored the need to collaborate with educators and trainers when crafting teaching assistance tools as a prerequisite for both seamless AI integration into pedagogical practices and its general wider acceptance. Beyond individual proficiency, the effective utilisation of AI in learning support requires a broader reconfiguration of tools, fostering an ergonomic evolution that aligns with the dynamic needs of stakeholders.

In conclusion, through the studies presented, this chapter highlights the challenges of integrating AI into vocational training: the difficulties of quality data collection and dealing with the complex interplay between technological developments, collaborative efforts, and socio-technical dynamics. The journey forward demands a thoughtful and collaborative approach, navigating the evolving landscape of AI in education and professional learning.

## References

Albero, B. (2019). La théorie de l'enquête: relier les pôles épistémè et praxis de l'activité. *Recherche et formation, 92.* https://doi.org/10.4000/recherche formation.5651

Casilli, A.-A. (2019). *En attendant les robots. Enquête sur le travail du clic.* Seuil.

Chiron, T. (2018). *Explorer les potentialités d'un Environnement Virtuel Educatif (Silva Numerica) pour favoriser l'apprentissage de situations complexes et dynamiques en lien avec le vivant: le cas d'apprenants forestiers.* Colloque doctoral international de l'éducation et de la formation. Rennes, France. https://hal.science/hal-01767554

Chrétien, F., Métral, J.-F. & Olry, P. (2020). Voir ce qui ne se voit pas. Regarder, voir, savoir en fromagerie. *Revue d'Anthropologie des connaissances, 14*(3). http://journals.openedition.org/rac/10523, https://doi.org/10.4000/rac.10523

Ciavaldini-Cartaut, S., Métral J.-F., Olry, P., Guidoni-Stoltz, D. et Gagneur, C.-A. (2022). L'IA en formation professionnelle : usages, fiabilité des traces d'apprentissage et problèmes posés aux concepteurs et aux enseignants-formateurs. In Romero, M., Heiser, L. et Lepage, A. (Eds). Livre blanc

Enseigner et apprendre à l'ère de l'IA. Acculturation, intégration et usages créatifs de l'IA en éducation (pp. 63–75). Direction du numérique pour l'éducation. Ministère de l'éducation nationale de la jeunesse et des sports.

David, M., & Droyer, N. (2019). Evaluation de la co-conception d'un environnement virtuel éducatif forestier - Pré-enquête à l'entrée par le critère de pertinence. *e-JIREF, 5*(3). http://journal.admee.org/index.php/ejiref/article/view/21

Dujarier, M. A. (2010). L'automatisation du jugement sur le travail. Mesurer n'est pas évaluer. *Cahiers internationaux de sociologie, 1*, 135–159.

Folcher, V., & Rabardel, P. (2004). 15. Hommes, artefacts, activités: perspective instrumentale. In *Ergonomie* (pp. 251–268). Presses Universitaires de France.

Gagneur, C.-A. & Vassout, D. (2019). *Étude garage connecté: usage des outils connectés*. Rapport de recherche dans le cadre d'un Projet d'Investissement d'Avenir (PIA). Association Nationale pour la Formation Automobile (ANFA). https://www.anfa-auto.fr/observatoire/la-prospective/competences-numeriques

Guidoni-Stoltz, D. (2019). *Concevoir un environnement virtuel éducatif pour «capitaliser», former ou développer l'intelligence professionnelle des forestiers: intérêts et (dés) illusions de la simulation*. Acte du colloque international de l'association Recherches et Pratiques en Didactique Professionnelle (RPDP). Université de Sherbrooke, Longueuil, Canada.

Guidoni-Stoltz, D. (2020). L'œil du forestier, instrument et miroir de l'activité professionnelle: Une perspective de didactique professionnelle. *Revue d'Anthropologie des connaissances, 14*(3). http://journals.openedition.org/rac/8371, https://doi.org/10.4000/rac.8371

Hwang, G.-J., Xie, H., Wah, B. W., & Gašević, D. (2020). Vision, challenges, roles and research issues of Artificial Intelligence in Education. *Computers and Education: Artificial Intelligence, 1*, 100001. https://doi.org/10.1016/j.caeai.2020.100001

Knight, S., & Buckingham, S. (2017). Theory and learning analytics. In C. Lang, G. Siemens, A. Wise, & G. Dragan (Eds.), *Handbook of learning analytics* (pp. 17–22). SOLAR. https://www.solaresearch.org/publications/hla-17/

Littlejohn, A. (2017). Learning and work: Professional learning analytics. In C. Lang, G. Siemens, A. Wise, & D. Gasevic (Eds.), *Handbook of learning analytics* (pp. 268–276). SOLAR. https://www.solaresearch.org/publications/hla-17

Mayen, P., & Lainé, A. (Eds.). (2014). *Apprendre à travailler avec le vivant ? Développement durable et didactique professionnelle*. Éditions Raison et Passions.

Savoyant, A. (2006). Tâche, activité et formation des actions de travail. *Éducation permanente, 166*, 127–136.

Vadcard, L. (2013). Étude didactique de la dialectique du travail et de la formation au bloc opératoire. *Éducation et didactique, 7*(1). https://doi.org/10.4000/educationdidactique.1598

Vadcard, L. (2019). *Vers une didactique des gestes techniques. Enjeux pour la formation professionnelle en santé*. Université de Bourgogne Franche-Comté.

**Open Access** This chapter is licensed under the terms of the Creative Commons Attribution 4.0 International License (http://creativecommons.org/licenses/by/4.0/), which permits use, sharing, adaptation, distribution and reproduction in any medium or format, as long as you give appropriate credit to the original author(s) and the source, provide a link to the Creative Commons license and indicate if changes were made.

The images or other third party material in this chapter are included in the chapter's Creative Commons license, unless indicated otherwise in a credit line to the material. If material is not included in the chapter's Creative Commons license and your intended use is not permitted by statutory regulation or exceeds the permitted use, you will need to obtain permission directly from the copyright holder.

# 12

# Manifesto in Defence of Human-Centred Education in the Age of Artificial Intelligence

Margarida Romero, Thomas Frosig, Amanda M. L. Taylor-Beswick, Jari Laru, Bastienne Bernasco, Alex Urmeneta, Oksana Strutynska, and Marc-André Girard

**Abstract** This manifesto advocates for the thoughtful integration of AI in education, emphasising a human-centred approach amid the rapid evolution of artificial intelligence (AI). The chapter explores the transformative potential of large language models (LLM) and generative AI (GenAI) in education, addressing both opportunities and concerns. While AI accelerates change in education, adapting to students'

---

M. Romero (✉) · T. Frosig · A. Urmeneta
Université Côte d'Azur, Nice, France
e-mail: margarida.romero@univ-cotedazur.fr; margarida.romero@unice.fr

T. Frosig
e-mail: thomas.frosig@etu.univ-cotedazur.fr

A. Urmeneta
e-mail: alex.urmeneta@etu.univ-cotedazur.fr

A. M. L. Taylor-Beswick
University of Cumbria, Carlisle, UK
e-mail: a.taylor-beswick@cumbria.ac.uk

diverse learning needs, it also poses challenges to traditional assessment paradigms. The manifesto stresses the importance of empowering teachers and students as decision-makers, highlighting the need for a balanced approach to AI integration. It emphasises human-centricity in AI use, promoting ethical considerations, responsible practices, and regulations. The right to choose and co-create is underscored, giving autonomy to educators and learners in selecting technologies aligned with their philosophies. Additionally, the manifesto introduces the concept of hybrid intelligence (HI), advocating collaboration between human and machine intelligence to enhance educational experiences. The manifesto encourages creative uses of AI in education, envisioning a harmonious partnership where AI and humans co-create transformative knowledge.

**Keywords** Human-centred education · Hybrid intelligence · Generative AI · AI education · Large language models

J. Laru
University of Oulu, Oulu, Finland
e-mail: jari.laru@oulu.fi

B. Bernasco
Saxion University of Applied Sciences, Enschede, The Netherlands
e-mail: s.h.c.m.bernasco@saxion.nl

O. Strutynska
Dragomanov Ukrainian State University, Kyiv, Ukraine
e-mail: o.v.strutynska@npu.edu.ua

M.-A. Girard
Université de Montréal, Montreal, QC, Canada
e-mail: marc-andre.girard.2@umontreal.ca

## Introduction

When the term AI first saw the light of day at the Dartmouth workshop in 1956, the proposal for the conference included the assertion that 'every aspect of learning or any other feature of intelligence can be so precisely described that a machine can be made to simulate it' (McCarthy et al., 2006, p. 12). In the past, the focus was on creating machines that could simulate learning and intelligence. However, the current discourse on AI in the public domain is shifting away from mere simulation towards acknowledging the significant disruption of human processes and practices that AI has set in motion. Indeed, one could encapsulate this disruption by highlighting the stark contrast between the rapid evolution of AI and the comparatively slower pace at which most educational actors are acquainting themselves to these advancements. Unlike every transformative technology before it, AI developments continue to move at speed and scale, allowing little time for acceptability and the subsequent and necessary mechanisms of overview and governance.

Traditional AI systems focused on narrow tasks, such as playing chess (Mainzer & Mainzer, 2020). In contrast, current foundation models possess a pre-trained, generalised knowledge base that enables them to perform a wide array of language-related tasks. This versatility positions foundation models as potential game-changers in education, in which learning is most often supported by linguistic interactions. Today's AI foundational models, defined as 'the base models trained on large-scale data in a self-supervised semi-supervised manner that can be adapted for several other downstream tasks' (Bommasani et al., 2021), are capable of simulating not only every neural aspect of learning but also a wide range of creative activities, solving complex problems, generating functional computer code, and quoting a majority of the authored world. These AI applications seek to produce a wide and general variety of outputs based on large linguistic models, which can be adapted to a range of educational interactions including information searches, creating exemplars, generating detailed explanations or summaries, language translations, creating quiz questions, and even simulating dialogue for interactive learning scenarios.

In this manifesto, we consider the UNICEF definition of AI, which is future-proof, human-oriented, and data-dependent (Holmes et al., 2022). AI refers to 'machine-based systems that can, given a set of human-defined objectives, make predictions, recommendations, or decisions that influence real or virtual environments' (OECD, 2019, para. 12). AI systems interact with us and act on our environment, either directly or indirectly. Often, they appear to operate autonomously, and can adapt their behaviour when provided additional context (UNICEF, 2021). In this chapter, special focus is put on the educational and societal impacts of large language models (LLM) and generative AI (GenAI) over more traditional AI technologies, such as machine learning (ML). In the following paragraphs, we use the generic term artificial intelligence (AI) for these separate artificial intelligence technologies.

The advanced capabilities of AI may be seductive as a potential technical solution for the educational system's shortcomings during the global school closures caused by the COVID-19 pandemic as well as the current educational challenges around diversity in the learning process. Through adaptive learning environments (Dogan et al., 2023; Minn, 2022), AI can identify and respond to students' unique learning challenges, preferences, and pace, fostering a more inclusive and effective educational environment. Similar to AI, the use of mobile technologies in the classroom has been discussed as both an opportunity, such as when it is used to support pedagogy or learning activities, as well as a distractor, in instances when it is applied without pedagogical strategies. As such, some schools have chosen to ban such devices or technologies in their codes of behaviour. In this context, the ongoing debates regarding the need to limit access to different types of technologies for K12 learners continue to highlight the concerns among educational stakeholders—notably parents, teachers, school principals, and policy makers—regarding its use. The integration of technology in school activities and curriculum remains a contentious issue in which technologists and technophobes provide different perspectives on a complex phenomenon where technology transformation creates both opportunities and challenges (Culver, 2017; Romero et al., 2016).

Likewise, AI accelerates the rate of change in different educational domains by developing models, enriched through machine learning, used to develop predictions or create educational content. This process can disrupt the standard assessment paradigm (SAP), as defined by Mislevy et al. (2012), by personalising the assessment process and allowing for more accurate and relevant measurements. Here AI excels at replicating educational elements, such as evaluation methods like multiple-choice questions, essays, and short-answer questions, while also supporting adaptive learning systems where learning analytics are used to support the learning process. However, it is important to note that AI cannot replicate every aspect of learning. For instance, when evaluating learning processes centred around a shared understanding or values fostering metacognition, as well as competency-based assessment of activities in which human empathy, morality, and subjectivity are required, AI tools are limited in their ability to develop real-sensitivity feedback, even if they can be designed to simulate a certain type of empathic relationship with the end-user (Montemayor et al., 2022). This underscores how AI is considered as an enhancement of teaching practices to augment the learning experience through a hybrid intelligence approach rather than a replacement of certain teaching tasks. Hence, while AI technologies provide enormous potential for the learner's experience and education in general, there is also sufficient cause for concerns (Dwivedi et al., 2023).

Another challenge of AI technologies deals with human creation and originality.

The integration of AI carries the potential for varying degrees of plagiarism and unethically facilitated collaborative creation of intellectual content. This ethical concern looms over both students and educators, encompassing not only the manner in which students use AI, but also the guidance provided by their teachers (Dwivedi et al., 2023). The intellectual property challenges in the use of generative AI have led to different research journals, newspapers, and Higher Education Institutions setting up guidelines for regulating the ethical use of AI in the human production of new works.

This manifesto advocates for a balanced and thoughtful integration of AI technology into the educational landscape. It does this by recognising the current tensions between AI's inherent potential and its ability to disrupt the current human-centred education paradigm. It also seeks to distance itself from the often polarising debate where AI is either a transformative solution with the ability to greatly benefit education or an unpredictable technology, controlled by powerful companies with hidden motives. While both sides may yet hold some truth, by focusing solely on AI's underlying technology, we risk losing sight of the very essence of education: the support of human development and well-being within a community.

In the following sections, the learning scientists and education experts behind this manifesto present several recommendations to help mitigate the scale of AI's disruption in educational settings. Our hope is that these recommendations provide context to educational stakeholders and developers seeking guidance on how to integrate AI technology, while retaining teacher and student agency and supporting, rather than displacing, future teaching and learning processes. Finally, we acknowledge that these recommendations, presented here at the dawn of AI's adoption, will need to evolve in order to keep pace with this rapidly changing technology.

# Empowering Students and Teachers as Decision-Makers

Cuban (1986) recognises that one of the main challenges associated with integrating technology into education is the exclusion of teachers in the decision-making process. Involving teachers in the participatory design process and empowering them to adapt the technology to the needs of their students is indispensable for ensuring that developed learning solutions align with their needs and the needs of their learners (Frøsig, 2023). Tedre et al. (2023) propose a similar approach with their project to engage Finnish students in a collaborative machine learning design process. Teachers are an essential component of the learning process in a human-centred educational system because they help students develop a common knowledge of their roles and duties based on a distinct purpose and core set of values. This relationship, based on collaboration and shared goals, is an essential component of education.

However, the prevailing trend in educational technology to prioritise automated indicators, even though they can miss aspects of the learning experience not easily represented by data, can sometimes lead to learning analytics being emphasised at the expense of pedagogic principles and ethics (Williamson, 2022). For example, factors such as socio-economic status, values, and motivations can be difficult to quantify using data, but play a substantial role in a learner's progress, nonetheless. Sahlberg and Hasak (2017) argue that mining for Big Data can divert educators, leaders, pundits, and policymakers from meeting the diverse and unique needs of their students. As such, they promote the use of 'Small Data' (Lindstrom, 2016) to underline 'small clues that uncover huge trends' (Sahlberg & Hasak, 2017, p. 7), typically centred on students' progress, emotions, behaviours, and other important observable details.

To enable meaningful integration, educational technologies should empower teachers to make informed choices, not only within their classrooms, but also at the national level. As Sahlberg and Hasak (2017) advocate, this can be achieved by giving more autonomy to the educators, aiming for an emancipation from school bureaucracy. It is imperative to reverse the current trend of surrendering decision-making power to technologies and, instead, place educators at the forefront when shaping the educational journey of students (Tedre et al., 2023). Learning is a social process and, currently, only humans can process the full spectrum of observable and unobservable factors that impact student learning. Furthermore, sidelining teachers runs the risk of excluding a substantial body of professional expertise and longitudinal knowledge regarding their learners. Additionally, teachers can act as a counterbalance to an over reliance on learning analytics where machine technology and its outputs are automatically assumed to be correct (Swiecki et al., 2022).

## Impact of Artificial Intelligence on Existing Educational Paradigms

The widespread availability of technologies, such as generative AI, poses a significant challenge to traditional pedagogical instruction-based practices and assessment methodologies. While the current educational systems in most of the member Organisation for Economic Co-operation and Development (OECD) countries focus on evaluating student performance based on their ability to meet specific learning goals, there are initiatives afoot that seek to put student engagement and agency above the role of learning goals (Harouni, 2015).

The current evolution of AI agents is moving them beyond text-based interactions towards multimodal collaboration where AI is seen as a partner rather than merely a tool. Here AI can assume the role of either a coach or a teammate, which can support self-regulation, collaboration, knowledge co-construction, and problem solving (Cress & Kimmerle, 2023; Dwivedi et al., 2023; Lodge et al., 2023; Mollick & Mollick, 2023; Sharples, 2023).

Contemporary AI technologies can be considered as an extension of existing knowledge and skills, which extends and enhances in ways that go beyond what either a human or machine could do individually. More precisely, such technologies can be integrated into the thinking and learning processes students engage in. For example, AI image generators can potentially enhance and build on human capabilities for creativity (Lodge et al., 2023).

Furthermore, Sharples (2023) introduced several ideas of how contemporary Generative AI tools could be used to scaffold students in collaborative and dialogical learning: (a) generator of possibilities; (b) opponent in argumentation; (c) an assistant in design; (d) an exploratory tool; (e) collaborator in creative writing. However, because the reliability and accuracy of information provided by generative AI is not guaranteed, metacognitive skills like self-reflection and critical thinking are needed when students work with generative AI. In practice, human learners need to self-monitor their learning goals and states, continuously evaluate AI responses, and adapt their own learning strategies or prompts to AI (Lodge et al., 2023). Evaluating responses is a complex skill in itself. It requires students to compare responses by AI to scientifically or expertly grounded responses, and to evaluate how relevant the AI responses are to the context of the problem.

From a future perspective, designing AI that can fully participate as an agent in social learning activities and fine-tune existing language models for educational purposes is not an adequate approach. According to Sharples (2023), current AI technologies lack, for example, 'long-term memory, the ability to reflect on its output and consolidate its knowledge from each conversation. More fundamentally, it does not capture the affective and experiential aspects of what it takes to be a learner and teacher' (p. 7).

Likewise, it is also important to start considering how UX, in the framework of co-creative AI systems (CAIS), might encourage, or even discourage, new modes of human–AI co-creativity by virtue of its interactive design (Feldman, 2017). The idea of a text box being the ideal gateway to AI for the majority of users and use cases already seems dated. It will be interesting to see how users might perceive AI differently when engaged in a 'spoken conversation' versus words typed in a text box (Rezwana & Maher, 2021). Given its ability to impact the cognitive and emotional factors in human–AI interactions, there is a need to support further UX analysis and development for improving AI technologies in education.

## Artificial Intelligence in Human-Centred Education

In advocacy of a human-centred approach to education, it is essential to establish frameworks that guide the ethical and responsible use of AI technologies. Creating these frameworks requires an ongoing dialogue between educators, learners, AI developers, technologists, legislators, and other stakeholders with the expressed purpose of creating alignment between the means (e.g. technology or pedagogy) and the objectives (e.g. the purpose of education) of its use. AI can be viewed as a tool for achieving specific goals, but those goals should be clearly defined, shared among all stakeholders, and transparent in purpose. Within this context, the European Union's (EU) recent AI Act takes the first steps in creating a legally binding framework for the regulation of AI's development and use in its member states. Importantly, one of the primary stated goals of the EU's AI Act is that AI systems should be overseen by people, rather than being automated, recognising the role humans play in guiding its use and preventing harmful outcomes (Helberger & Diakopoulos, 2023; Kazim et al., 2023).

Given its potential for disruption, teachers should have the autonomy to reject certain technologies that may not align with their pedagogical philosophy or the unique needs of their students. Simultaneously, learners should be granted the right to explore and test emerging technologies under the guidance of educators. This dual approach respects the agency of both teachers and learners, fostering an environment where educational technologies are not imposed, but collaboratively chosen based on their merit and relevance. While teachers should be empowered to reject certain technologies, learners should also have the right to benefit from different technologies that might support their learning and co-creative processes.

To support this aim, teachers will need access to ongoing professional development in the form of multi-disciplinary training groups and dynamic learning communities. Romero (2023) argues that this calls for a simultaneous focus on improving teachers' digital competences as well as the time and space necessary to allow for their acculturation to AI. Access to diverse types of acculturation activities is critical if teachers are to develop the confidence and agency necessary to gauge the impact of rapidly evolving technologies. For instance, participation in dynamic learning communities can help teachers develop a diversity of expertises that benefit not only their classrooms, but the school and wider community at large. Furthermore, participation in these learning communities can benefit teachers by giving them access to peers whose specific digital competencies might scaffold their own inherent weaknesses. This also serves to benefit learners who, without this framework of shared expertise, may not have had access to certain technologies such as educational robotics, artificial intelligence, maker education, or creative programming. Continuous professional development also plays a key role in ensuring that teachers are prepared for potential disruptions caused by AI in education. Given the speed at which AI technologies are advancing, ongoing professional training will be key to ensuring that teachers have access to the latest pedagogical methods and materials as well as continuous updates on the technology's evolution. Additionally, co-design activities between researchers, learners, and educators should not only be encouraged, but proactively initiated and supported through curriculum, dedicated learning environments, and research partnerships.

An example of such an activity can be found in Finland with the Generation AI[1] project, which aims to empower teachers and students by increasing their data agency and AI literacy through the use of co-created AI tools, materials, and pedagogies.

## Hybrid Intelligence

Akata et al. (2020) introduce hybrid intelligence (HI) as a paradigm that combines human and machine intelligence to enhance human intellect and capabilities, emphasising collaboration rather than replacement. In formulating a research agenda for HI, they identify four key challenges, including Collaborative HI, Adaptive HI, Responsible HI, and Explainable HI. These challenges underscore the need to address the intricate dynamics between humans and intelligent systems, laying the foundation for the evolution of AI technologies. The emphasis on collaboration between AI and humans within hybrid intelligence aligns with the idea of empowering individuals to actively engage with AI systems towards a defined objective. Additionally, the pursuit of adaptive intelligence supports an individuals' capacity to learn and adapt to evolving technological landscapes, as facilitated by improved data and AI literacy.

In contemplating the potential of hybrid intelligence to augment human capabilities through technology, it is essential to consider the foundational human resources that have been instrumental in the development of AI. The agentic use of AI, as highlighted by the emphasis on data and AI literacy, serves to bridge the gap between AI's technological potential and the capacity to develop new activities and products. By nurturing the ability to comprehend and navigate the complexities of data and artificial intelligence, learners can become active participants in the development and utilisation of AI. This objective aligns seamlessly with the overarching goal of augmenting human capabilities, emphasising the empowerment of individuals to make informed decisions and

---

[1] Generation AI project: https://www.generation-ai-stn.fi.

contributions in a technology-driven landscape. These types of participatory approaches can also support the development of the agentic uses of AI (Tedre et al., 2023).

These participatory approaches become a pivotal aspect in addressing the challenges set forth by Akata et al. (2020) and implemented in the workshops by Tedre et al. (2020). It not only aligns with the goals of Collaborative and Adaptive HI, but also reinforces the importance of foundational human sources in shaping the trajectory of hybrid intelligence. The development of data and AI literacy is not just an objective, but a catalyst for allowing learners to benefit from AI with the possibility to develop different applications of hybrid intelligence in education.

Lodge et al. (2023) refer to hybrid learning as an educational approach where generative AI systems work in conjunction with human learners in order to promote both cognitive and metacognitive aspects of learning. From a cognitive perspective, AI technologies can be used to scaffold instances of information processing, content generation, or problem solving. Similarly, AI from a metacognitive perspective can support learners with features like real-time feedback, adaptive questioning, and self-assessment prompts helping learners to monitor, evaluate, and adjust their learning strategies. This makes AI an active interlocutor or teammate (Lodge et al., 2023).

# Creative Uses of Artificial Intelligence in Education

Beyond conventional uses of AI as a tool for generating text, image, or content, AI emerges as a dynamic force not only for co-creating knowledge in participatory settings, but also for reshaping human practices. This transcendent use of AI for good (#AI4good) involves a paradigm shift, where AI tools engage in a shared, collaborative process with human agents, contributing to the conceptualization and development of critical knowledge (Septiani et al., 2023). At this pinnacle, AI is seamlessly integrated into the creation of transformative knowledge, fostering agency, and catalysing a profound evolution in human practices (Romero, 2023). It is here that humans and AI cohabitate, playing

## 12 Manifesto in Defence of Human-Centred Education … 

to each other's strengths, with each lending qualities that individually make them unique, but together true collaborators (Wu et al., 2021).

Figure 12.1, showing the six levels of the #PPAI6 model, presents a way of differentiating between the different types of creative engagement in human–AI activities (Romero, 2023). This model provides a continuum that starts with passive consumption and evolves into more active and participatory forms of engagement, emphasising the diverse ways in which individuals and groups can collaborate with AI in the learning process.

- Level 1. Passive consumer: The learner consumes AI-generated content without understanding how it works.
- Level 2. Interactive consumer: The learner interacts with AI-generated content. The AI system adapts to the learners' actions.
- Level 3. Individual content creation: The learner creates new content using AI tools.
- Level 4. Collaborative content creation: A team creates new content using AI tools.
- Level 5. Participatory knowledge co-creation: A team creates content thanks to AI tools and the collaboration of stakeholders in a complex problem.
- Level 6. Expansive learning supported by AI: In formative interventions supported by AI, participants' agency may expand or transform problematic situations. AI tools can be used to help identify contradictions in complex problems and help generate concepts or artefacts to regulate conflicting stimuli and foster collective agency and action.

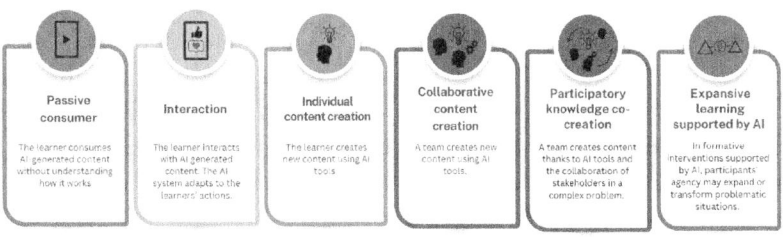

**Fig. 12.1** Six levels of creative engagement in human–AI in education

AI tools can be used to assist in the modelling of activity systems as well as in the simulation of new actions, facilitating the expansive visualisation process.

In order to support the agentic use of AI, levels 5 and 6 of the model are designed to contribute to learners' acculturation to AI and its fundamental principles. This strategic approach aims to empower learners, enabling their active engagement in participatory activities where hybrid intelligence flourishes through the synergistic collaboration of human–AI systems. These higher levels also aim to raise student and teacher awareness of AI through the lens of agentic and creative engagement.

In order to support agentic and creative engagement and establish new paradigms of human–AI co-creativity, more work will need to be done to address the challenges, latent or otherwise, to its acceptance. Foremost among these include displacement concerns, human biases towards AI created work, and the difficulty in applying value to AI co-creations given the subjective value assigned to creative works. Understanding creativity requires a nuanced consideration of specific cultural and human sensitivities, both in terms of their manifestation and evaluation. Consequently, as we contemplate human–AI co-creativity, it becomes imperative to explore the role of culture in shaping and influencing this collaborative process, understanding that it will need to navigate the same subjective, norm-aligned evaluation and value-assigned processes as other creativity projects. Likewise, Magni et al. (2023) highlight the phenomena of human gatekeeping where some forms of AI-produced work are assigned a lower value based on the perception of effort, or lack thereof. While there is research showing that anthropomorphic AI agents can moderate this producer-identify effect on the creative evaluation process (Glikson & Woolley, 2020; Israfilzade, 2023; Magni et al., 2023), further solutions will need to be found that counter the tendency for humans to ascribe value to effort or innate ability. Finally, there is a growing fear of displacement as humans wrestle with AI's impact on future workforce and professional opportunities (Thomson & Thomas, 2023; Tiwari, 2023).

At its pinnacle, the transformative potential of AI can transcend its role from knowledge co-creation to actively transforming human practices (Romero, 2023). At the highest level of creative engagement with the AI model (#PPAI6), AI is integrated into the creation of critical knowledge, fostering agency, and reshaping human practices. The collaborative process between generative AI tools and human agents becomes a shared endeavour to develop agency and enact transformative changes. This aligns seamlessly with the goal of expansive learning where formative interventions contribute to expanding or transforming problematic situations. AI tools, in this context, play a vital role in identifying contradictions, generating concepts, regulating conflicting stimuli, and ultimately fostering collective agency and action.

## Inclusivity and Diversity in Artificial Intelligence

The challenges in ethics and inclusivity arise due to the high complexity and diversity of cognitive technologies, including human–AI applications in education. The AI act developed at the European level has been a clear example of the level of complexity in creating consensus in AI principles that ensure citizens' rights while simultaneously supporting innovation. Attempts to align individual issues with stakeholders are hindered by the many tensions between stakeholder objectives. Interventions in one part of the AI ecosystem (e.g. need for learners' privacy) can have consequences in other parts (e.g. uses of facial recognition to identify the learners' engagements). These tensions require a participatory approach in the design of AI systems that could be developed for educational purposes (Holmes et al., 2021).

Stahl (2021) proposes three main requirements for interventions meant to improve the ethical design and integration of AI. Firstly, interventions need to clearly delineate the boundaries of the ecosystem (e.g. the educational actors engaged) in relation to the actors, but also the geographical scope and the topics addressed. Secondly, interventions should focus on knowledge development, support, maintenance, and dissemination within the AI ecosystems. In education, this raises the need for the different educational actors to develop an understanding of AI fundamentals and the way that human–AI collaboration can support the teaching and learning processes. Lastly, interventions need to be adaptive and flexible to emerging needs. In relation to inclusivity, there is a need to support pre-service and in-service teachers in their acculturation to the fundamentals of AI. This support will aid their decision-making process for the integration, or not, of AI technologies and allow them to consider the agentic and creative engagement learners can develop using these tools.

## Advancing Towards an Increased Human-Centred Education in the Age of AI

The challenges and opportunities presented in this manifesto highlight the need to develop critical thinking as well as an acculturation to AI for each of the varied educational stakeholders. In particular, developing critical thinking skills has become essential given the escalating challenges posed by AI integration in the educational and non-educational uses of Generative AI. These include, but are not limited to, generating fake information, unethical AI-generated content, and impersonations such as deep fakes. The proliferation of misinformation, across digital formats, has the potential to manipulate public opinion, incite conflicts on various grounds (e.g., racial, religious), and exacerbate existing inequalities and stereotypes such as gender disparities (Vartiainen et al., 2023). While students should be taught the skills necessary to recognise and dismiss fake information, there is also a need to regulate the type of AI content that could compromise students' privacy and integrity.

It is not just generative AI that impacts our students' everyday lives. AI is ubiquitous and pervasive (social media and mobile phones are examples), and often coupled with massive-scale data collection. This has given rise to a plethora of complex challenges and ethical dilemmas including uneven power relationships, privacy rights violations, total surveillance, hybrid influencing, behaviour engineering, and algorithmic biases (Page et al., 2022). Kahila et al. (submitted) acknowledge the computational processes changing the cultural practices and decision-making by individuals, organisations, and institutions and suggest the development of data agency as a solution to these societal challenges.

Educators face the crucial task of equipping citizens with the skills necessary to navigate a society permeated by AI systems and tools. In this context, fostering acculturation to AI from an early age, as part of an overarching digital literacy framework that includes critical thinking, emerges as a pivotal strategy. For this objective, the Digital Competence Framework for Citizens (DigComp 2.2) (Vuorikari et al., 2022) offers a comprehensive guide, encompassing elements tailored for interacting with AI systems. To bolster citizens' AI literacy, educators can leverage this framework as a foundation for planning and developing curricula and course materials. Furthermore, by integrating these competencies into educational practices, educators contribute to the cultivation of a digitally competent citizenry capable of discerning, evaluating, and navigating the intricate landscape of information in the age of AI.

In collaboration with the DigComp 2.2 framework, educators will also need to develop age appropriate tools and materials to ensure that students at every level have access to fundamental AI concepts. These AI competency frameworks are required to navigate the evolving landscape of education in the age of AI and support a human-centred approach to education as a major pillar of our educational systems. This manifesto calls for a re-evaluation of the current contradictions, emphasising the need to empower teachers, ethically regulate the use of transformative technologies, and uphold the rights of both educators and learners. By doing so, we can forge a path towards an educational future where technology complements and enhances the human experience rather than overshadowing it.

# References

Akata, Z., Balliet, D., De Rijke, M., Dignum, F., Dignum, V., Eiben, G., et al. (2020). A research agenda for hybrid intelligence: Augmenting human intellect with collaborative, adaptive, responsible, and explainable artificial intelligence. *Computer, 53*(8), 18–28.

Bommasani, R., Hudson, D. A., Adeli, E., Altman, R., Arora, S., von Arx, S., et al. (2021). *On the opportunities and risks of foundation models.* arXiv preprint arXiv:2108.07258

Cress, U., & Kimmerle, J. (2023). Co-constructing knowledge with generative AI tools: Reflections from a CSCL perspective. *International Journal of Computer-Supported Collaborative Learning.* https://doi.org/10.1007/s11412-023-09409-w

Cuban, L. (1986). *Teachers and machines: The classroom use of technology since 1920.* Teachers College Press.

Culver, B. L. (2017). *Technology in education: Technology integration into the school's curriculum* (doctoral dissertation). Trident University International, Cypress, CA.

Dogan, M. E., Goru Dogan, T., & Bozkurt, A. (2023). The use of artificial intelligence (AI) in online learning and distance education processes: A systematic review of empirical studies. *Applied Sciences, 13*(5), 3056.

Dwivedi, Y. K., Kshetri, N., Hughes, L., Slade, E. L., Jeyaraj, A., Kar, A. K., et al. (2023). "So what if ChatGPT wrote it?" Multidisciplinary perspectives on opportunities, challenges and implications of generative conversational AI for research, practice and policy. *International Journal of Information Management, 71*, 102642.

Feldman, S. S. (2017, July). Co-creation: Human and AI collaboration in creative expression. In *Electronic Visualisation and the Arts* (EVA 2017). BCS Learning & Development.

Frøsig, T. B. (2023). Expanding the Technology Acceptance Model (TAM) to consider teachers needs and concerns in the design of Educational Technology (EdTAM). *International Journal of Emerging Technologies in Learning, 18*(16), 130–140.

Glikson, E., & Woolley, A. (2020, March 12). Human trust in artificial intelligence: Review of empirical research. *The Academy of Management Annals.* https://doi.org/10.5465/annals.2018.0057.

Harouni, H. (2015). *Purpose and education: The case of mathematics* (Doctoral dissertation). Harvard Graduate School of Education.

Helberger, N., & Diakopoulos, N. (2023). ChatGPT and the AI act. *Internet Policy Review, 12*(1). https://doi.org/10.14763/2023.1.1682

Holmes, W., Persson, J., Chounta, I. A., Wasson, B., & Dimitrova, V. (2022). *Artificial intelligence and education: A critical view through the lens of human rights, democracy and the rule of law.* Council of Europe.

Holmes, W., Porayska-Pomsta, K., Holstein, K., Sutherland, E., Baker, T., Shum, S. B., Santos, O. C., Rodrigo, M. T., Cukurova, M., Bittencourt, I. I., & Koedinger, K. R. (2021). Ethics of AI in education: Towards a community-wide framework. *International Journal of Artificial Intelligence in Education, 32*, 504–526.

Israfilzade, K. (2023). *Beyond automation: The impact of anthropomorphic generative AI on conversational marketing*. 8th International European Conference on Interdisciplinary Scientific Research, Vol. 5, No. 2, pp. 757–766.

Kahila, J., Vartiainen, H., Tedre, M., Arkko, E., Lin, A., Pope, N., Jormanainen, I., & Valtonen, T. (submitted). *Pedagogical framework for cultivating children's data agency and creative abilities in the age of AI*.

Kazim, E., Güçlütürk, O., Almeida, D., Kerrigan, C., Lomas, E., Koshiyama, A., et al. (2023). Proposed EU AI act—Presidency compromise text: Select overview and comment on the changes to the proposed regulation. *AI and Ethics, 3*(2), 381–387.

Lindstrom, M. (2016). *Small data: The tiny clues that reveal huge trends*. Martin's Press.

Lodge, J., Yang, S., Furze, L., & Dawson, P. (2023). It's not like a calculator, so what is the relationship between learners and generative artificial intelligence? *Learning: Research and Practice, 9*(2), 117–124. https://doi.org/10.1080/23735082.2023.2261106

Magni, F., Park, J., & Chao, M. M. (2023). Humans as creativity gatekeepers: Are we biased against AI creativity? *Journal of Business and Psychology*, 1–14.

Mainzer, K., & Mainzer, K. (2020). A short history of the AI. In *Artificial intelligence—When do machines take over?* (pp. 7–13). Springer.

McCarthy, J., Minsky, M. L., Rochester, N., & Shannon, C. E. (2006). A proposal for the Dartmouth summer research project on artificial intelligence, August 31, 1955. *AI Magazine, 27*(4), 12. https://doi.org/10.1609/aimag.v27i4.1904

Minn, S. (2022). AI-assisted knowledge assessment techniques for adaptive learning environments. *Computers and Education: Artificial Intelligence, 3*, 100050.

Mislevy, R. J., Behrens, J. T., Dicerbo, K. E., & Levy, R. (2012). Design and discovery in educational assessment: Evidence-centered design, psychometrics, and educational data mining. *Journal of Educational Data Mining, 4*(1), 11–48. https://doi.org/10.5281/zenodo.3554641

Mollick, E. R., & Mollick, L. (2023). Assigning AI: Seven approaches for students, with prompts. *SSRN*. https://ssrn.com/abstract=4475995

Montemayor, C., Halpern, J., & Fairweather, A. (2022). In principle obstacles for empathic AI: Why we can't replace human empathy in healthcare. *AI & Society, 37*(4), 1353–1359.

OECD. (2019). *Recommendation of the Council on Artificial Intelligence*. OECD Legal Instruments. https://legalinstruments.oecd.org/en/instruments/oecd-legal-0449

Page, X., Berrios, S., Wilkinson, D., & Wisniewski, P. J. (2022). Social media and privacy. In B. P. Knijnenburg, X. Page, P. Wisniewski, H. R. Lipford, N. Proferes, & J. Romano (eds.), *Modern socio-technical perspectives on privacy* (pp. 113–147). Springer International Publishing.

Rezwana, J., & Maher, M. L. (2021). *COFI: A framework for modeling interaction in human-AI co-creative systems*. ICCC, pp. 444–448.

Romero, M. (2023). *Lifelong learning challenges in the era of artificial intelligence: A computational thinking perspective*. 12th International Research Meeting in Business and Management.

Romero, M., Laferriere, T., & Power, T. M. (2016). The move is on! From the passive multimedia learner to the engaged co-creator. *ELearn, 2016*(3). https://doi.org/10.1145/2904374.2893358

Sahlberg, P., & Hasak, J. (2017). Small data for big change. *Education: Journal of the N.S.W. Public School Teachers Federation, 98*(1), 7.

Septiani, D. P., Kostakos, P., & Romero, M. (2023, July). Analysis of creative engagement in AI tools in education based on the# PPai6 framework. In *International conference in methodologies and intelligent systems for technology enhanced learning* (pp. 48–58). Springer.

Sharples, M. (2023). Towards social generative AI for education: Theory, practices and ethics. *Learning: Research and Practice, 9*(2), 159–167, https://doi.org/10.1080/23735082.2023.2261131

Stahl, B. C. (2021). A*rtificial intelligence for a better future: An ecosystem perspective on the ethics of AI and emerging digital technologies* (p. 124). Springer Nature.

Swiecki, Z., Khosravi, H., Chen, G., Martinez-Maldonado, R., Lodge, J. M., Milligan, S., et al. (2022). Assessment in the age of artificial intelligence. *Computers and Education: Artificial Intelligence, 3*, 100075.

Tedre, M., Mäkitalo, K., Vartiainen, H., Kahila, J., Laru, J., & Iwata, M. (2023, June). *Generation AI: Participatory machine learning co-design projects with K-9 students in Finland*. Proceedings of the 2023 Conference on Innovation and Technology in Computer Science Education, 2, pp. 657–657.

Tedre, M., Vartiainen, H., Kahila, J., Toivonen, T., Jormanainen, I., & Valtonen, T. (2020, October). Machine learning introduces new perspectives to data agency in K—12 computing education. In *2020 IEEE Frontiers in Education Conference (FIE)* (pp. 1–8). IEEE.

Thomson, T. J., & Thomas, R. (2023, December 12). Generative visual AI in newsrooms: Considerations related to production, presentation, and audience interpretation and impact. *Journalism Research, 6*, 318–328. https://doi.org/10.1453/2569-152X-3_42023-13639-en

Tiwari, R. (2023, January 19). The impact of AI and machine learning on job displacement and employment opportunities. *International Journal of Engineering Technologies and Management Research, 7*. https://doi.org/10.55041/IJSREM17506

UNICEF. (2021). Policy guidance on AI for children 2.0. https://www.unicef.org/globalinsight/media/2356/file/UNICEF-Global-Insight-policy-guidance-AI-children-2.0-2021.pdf

Vartiainen, H., Kahila, J., Tedre, M., Sointu, E., & Valtonen, T. (2023). More than fabricated news reports: Children's perspectives and experiences of fake news. *Journal of Media Literacy Education, 15*(2), 17–30. https://doi.org/10.23860/JMLE-2023-15-2-2

Vuorikari, R., Kluzer, S., & Punie, Y. (2022). *DigComp 2.2: The digital competence framework for citizens—With new examples of knowledge, skills and attitudes* (EUR 31006 EN). Publications Office of the European Union. ISBN 978-92-76-48883-5. https://doi.org/10.2760/490274, JRC128415.

Williamson, B. (2022). Big EdTech. *Learning, Media and Technology, 47*(2), 157–162.

Wu, Z., Ji, D., Yu, K., Zeng, X., Wu, D., & Shidujaman, M. (2021). AI creativity and the human-AI co-creation model. In M. Kurosu (Ed.), *Human-computer interaction. Theory, methods and tools. HCII 2021.* Lecture Notes in Computer Science (Vol. 12762). Springer. https://doi.org/10.1007/978-3-030-78462-1_13

**Open Access** This chapter is licensed under the terms of the Creative Commons Attribution 4.0 International License (http://creativecommons.org/licenses/by/4.0/), which permits use, sharing, adaptation, distribution and reproduction in any medium or format, as long as you give appropriate credit to the original author(s) and the source, provide a link to the Creative Commons license and indicate if changes were made.

The images or other third party material in this chapter are included in the chapter's Creative Commons license, unless indicated otherwise in a credit line to the material. If material is not included in the chapter's Creative Commons license and your intended use is not permitted by statutory regulation or exceeds the permitted use, you will need to obtain permission directly from the copyright holder.

# Index

**A**

Acculturation to AI 46, 53, 76, 78, 85, 86, 104
Actionable feedback 120
Action-research 112
Adaptive algorithms 37
Adaptive learning 37
Affordances 118–120
Agency 173
Agency and predictive technologies 25–28
AI algorithms 64
AI and ethics 59, 60
AI governance 64
AI image generators 164
AI in education 4, 21, 22, 77
AI in higher education 12
AI initiatives 86, 97
AI in learning aids 30
AI integration 86, 152, 153
AI outreach 81, 82
AI's impact 78, 94, 149, 170
AI's impact on teaching and learning 29
AI technologies 160, 161
AI tutor 136
Assessment 161
Automation 110
Automation bias 24
Autonomy 163

**C**

Chatbots 135, 137, 138
ChatGPT 131, 132, 139
Citizen education 40
Citizenship 173
Civic education 105, 106
Computer-supported collaborative learning (CSCL) 12

Constraints of AI 53
Creative pedagogies 10, 12, 47
Creative uses of artificial intelligence 168
Critical situations 149
Critical thinking 103, 105

D
Data 110
Data models 130
Data privacy 133
Decision making 162
Definition of AI 21
Delegating mechanisable tasks 42
Developing ethical AI tools 29
Digital citizenship 58
Digital competencies 166
Digital game-based learning (DGBL) 122
Diversity 171

E
Educational serious games 10
Ethical challenges 66
Expansive learning supported by AI 9, 169

F
Feedback 136

G
Gamification 123
Gender bias 60, 91
Gender perspectives 83
Generative AI (GAI) 80, 130, 164

Generative AI tools 7
Governance 64

H
Healthcare 110
Higher Education (HE) 102–104, 130
Human agency 19
Human-AI collaboration 7, 8
Human-centred education 161, 162, 165, 172
Hybrid intelligence (HI) 167, 168

I
Immersive learning 125
Institutional applications 10
Integrating AI 40
Integration of digital technologies 49
Intelligent tutors 150, 152

K
KidLearn Project 37

L
Language learning 134, 136
Large language models (LLM) 160
Learning analytics 39, 123, 124, 146–148, 151
Learning community 166

M
Machine learning 162
Medical 110
Middle school 82

Middle schoolers 102
Middle students 106
Misuse of learning data 38
MOOCs and AI literacy 40

Participatory approaches 168
Participatory knowledge co-creation 9
Passive consumer 169
Passive-Participatory model 8
Pedagogical affordances 119
Personalisation 125
Perspectives on AI 106
Preserving agency 25
Problem-based learning 120
Professional development 49, 94
Professional didactics 147
Professional training 146
Professional use of digital technology 50

Recommendations for AI integration 29
Responsible use of AI 139
Risk of Overreliance on Algorithms/ Algorithms Limiting Agency 26
Robots 109–111

Science, technology, engineering, arts, and mathematics (STEAM) 91, 92, 105
Simulation 149, 150
Social affordances 121, 122
Societal impact 63
Student agency 23, 25, 82, 162
Student perspective 96
Students 108, 109
Students' voice 26
Sustainable development 84, 109

Teacher agency 23
Technical affordances 124
Technical system theory 20
Technician system 19
Techno-solutionism 5
Text-generative AI 132
Tokenisation 137
Transdiscplinary research 40
Transformation 171

Visualisation 124
Vocational training 146, 153

**SPRINGER NATURE**

## GPSR Compliance

*The European Union's (EU) General Product Safety Regulation (GPSR) is a set of rules that requires consumer products to be safe and our obligations to ensure this.*

*If you have any concerns about our products, you can contact us on ProductSafety@springernature.com*

In case Publisher is established outside the EU, the EU authorized representative is:

Springer Nature Customer Service Center GmbH
Europaplatz 3
69115 Heidelberg, Germany

The manufacturer's authorised representative in the EU is Springer Nature Customer Service Centre GmbH, Europaplatz 3, 69115 Heidelberg, Germany. If you have any concerns regarding our products, please contact ProductSafety@springernature.com

Printed and bound by CPI Group (UK) Ltd, Croydon, CR0 4YY

23/03/2026

02076447-0004